Disclaimer

This book is designed for educational purposes only. The services of a competent professional trainer or applied behaviorist should be sought regarding its applicability with respect to your own dog. The training of dogs is not without risk. The author and publisher shall have neither liability nor responsibility to any person or entity with respect to any loss or damage caused or alleged to be caused directly or indirectly by the information contained in this book.

If you do not wish to be bound by the above, you may return this book to the publisher for a full refund.

D1636705

ISBN 978-0-9705629-6-8

FIGHT!

A Guide to Dog-Dog Aggression

Contents

SECTION 2 DESCRIPTIONS OF COMMON TYPES

SECTION 3: ASSESSING PROGNOSIS

SECTION 4: REMEDIAL SOCIALIZATION FOR DOGS WITH IMPOVERISHED PLAY HISTORIES ("TARZAN")

SECTION 7: PLAY STYLE AND PLAY SKILLS

FIGHT!

A Guide to Dog-Dog Aggression

Introduction

This manual is about dogs who fight with, lunge at and don't get along with other dogs. It's a common problem, cropping up in a variety of contexts.

The first section explores the roots of dog social behavior, the paradigms currently put forward to interpret it and the enormously popular issue of environmental vs. genetic influences on behavior.

The second section describes common presentations of dog-dog aggression and how to tell them apart for treatment purposes. Classification of dog aggression into types is a virtual obsession with many camps within the dog behavior field, with literally scores of diagnostic categories ready for labeling any given case. This manual will present fewer categories, largely based on the principal cocktail of behavior modification techniques used to resolve them.

This emphasis on a classification system based on techniques that have been shown to resolve these problems refers to my behaviorist approach. I am defining behaviorism here as the observation and quantification of what animals *do* and how this can be influenced by the altering of stimulus-stimulus relationships – Pavlovian or Classical Conditioning – and response-consequence relationships – Skinnerian or Operant conditioning.

Although occasionally there will be some speculation and inference about what might be happening inside the dog – emotions, thoughts and motivations – I will emphasize what the dog is doing, and then focus on what consequences and associations can be manipulated to get him to do it more or do it less or to do something else altogether. Aggression is behavior like any other behavior, although often with greater emotional load for humans.

The third section begins with prognosis estimates – which cases can we reasonably expect to resolve and with what degree of confidence? Then the nuts and bolts of techniques are presented for each type of aggression.

Finally, I'll lay out a standard prevention program for use with puppies and for adults without problems.

Aggression – Normal or Abnormal Behavior?

To say that aggression is very prevalent in animals is an extreme understatement. Most days of their lives, animals defend themselves from perceived threat, compete over resources, try to obtain lunch and try to avoid becoming lunch. Animals without capacities for normal levels of aggression are summarily purged from the gene pool. Like fear, aggression is "good" in nature, insofar as it enhances survival and reproduction chances.

The problem with the companion dogs in our lives begins with the presumption that domestication has successfully obliterated all aggression, except pathological exceptions.

While dogs with neurological problems, endocrine imbalances and other bona fide organic abnormalities may behave aggressively as a result, the vast majority of aggression in domestic dogs would be highly adaptive in a natural context. The fact that aggression has not been purged from the domestic dog gene pool could be a result of breeding practices, the inherent difficulty in removing so vital a capacity, or both. Sub-optimal rearing practices, training and husbandry may then conspire to make things worse.

Ritualization: Are They Trying to Kill Each Other?

Another important factor to consider is our general failure to make a distinction between aggression that is ritualized and that which is not. In ritualized aggressive encounters, a "truthful" outcome will be obtained – the animal who would have won in a real contest wins – but without the very expensive ordeal of flat-out, no-punches-pulled aggression. Ritualization is highly advantageous to both participants, as this cost – high injury risk and energy expenditure - is borne by both winners and losers in a real contest.

We humans have a nicely developed understanding of ritualization in our own society. Take boxing, which is basically an aggressive encounter between two men in their prime. There are rules about where and how the combatants can punch, rules about who is considered the "winner" without having to maim or kill the other, they wear gloves with precise specifications, opponents must be of similar weight, and a referee watches the entire proceedings for rule infractions and to ensure that it is terminated prior to death or maiming injury.

Humans also appreciate the difference between filing a lawsuit and brandishing a machine gun. It is no different with animals: because aggression is so expensive and yet so necessary, all kinds of rituals have evolved. In the case of ritualized dog fights, the combatants will bite with non-maiming force, they will direct most bites at face, head, neck, withers and back, they will make horrific noises and faces, and usually rear up on hind legs. Neither terribly efficient nor effective if the goal was to kill the other dog, although most people witnessing dogfights are so impressed with the noise and visual spectacle that they assume this must be the case.

Indeed, most owners find even the most normal and ritualized levels of aggression distressing to witness. Their goal is to have no aggression of even the most ritualized sort delivered even in normal contexts. This is the equivalent of me requiring you to go through to the end of your life without ever once losing your temper and saying something a bit mean to a loved one, honking your horn at someone who cuts you off in traffic or writing a letter of complaint.

This is not to say that we should just let dogs "work it out," and refrain from intervening with behavior modification. The "let them work it out" piece of advice is a potentially damaging one and is trotted out far too often by well-meaning owners and trainers. There are cases where the use of remedial socialization – i.e. carefully selected dogs acting as the primary deliverers of operant contingencies and classical associations – can play a key role, and other cases where this should not be employed. There are other times when the option of complete non-intervention exists. But these are useful options for only some types of problems. In other kinds of cases, such approaches would be unhelpful and even detrimental.

The Behaviorist Model

Dog training and behavior modification is a field full of camps with different biases. One well-known distinction is that between trainers who use primarily or exclusively techniques that are free of aversives such as pain and startle and those who insist that aversives are necessary and benign. Another less well-publicized difference is whether one's focus is on observable data or on interpretations of what might be going on inside the dog's mind. This is the distinction between the behaviorist viewpoint and traditional dog training. Where a behaviorist is interested in observable and quantifiable behavior, a traditional trainer will offer interpretations about what the dog is thinking, his motives and his presumed status. The other contrasting model to behaviorism is the medical model, which is oriented toward symptom-diagnosis-treatment.

Where the medical model might see observable behavior as a *symptom* of an underlying problem, syndrome or illness, the behaviorist sticks to what the dog is *doing* – for instance, attacking other dogs in such and such a context – and modifies that behavior without attempts at guessing what is going on "in the black box." I can't know what is going on in the mind of any dog at any time. I can, however, see, measure and modify behavior using well-established principles of operant and classical conditioning. So, what you will find in this manual will be mostly descriptions of behavior and techniques for modifying that behavior. This is not to say that I don't have opinions or often have an entertaining time speculating about what I *think* is going on in a dog's head. It's just that, when it comes to behavior modification, a disciplined focus on what the dog is doing (or not doing) is usually more fruitful.

Nature Vs. Nurture

We are all fascinated with the question of whether a given behavior or personality trait is due to genetics or environment. Am I a compulsive house-cleaner because I carry a gene(s) that predisposes me to do OCD-related actions to manage anxiety or regulate the serotonin in my brain? Was it modeled for me in early life? Did it get paid off over the course of my life? Do I have a stress-mediated neurochemical imbalance? Are there multiple influences? Likewise, we are intrigued to know whether our dogs are a bit testy with other dogs because it is their nature – meaning genetic predisposition - or because of something that happened to them, such as bad experiences or impoverished socialization.

Science has looked at exactly these types of questions using such tools as identical twin studies and an ever-deeper understanding of DNA and newer disciplines like evolutionary psychology. It's all fascinating stuff. However, the important point in a discussion of dog aggression is the tendency of dog trainers to invoke one or the other explanation for problem behaviors *depending on whether they have the means to modify them.* In other words, if I can change behavior, it must therefore be wholly or predominantly learned or environmentally installed. If I can't, well, it must be genetic. It's a convenient misuse of the concept to get oneself off the hook. The fallacy is that even if these assessments were accurate about the preponderance of genetics or environmental influence on a given behavior, *it is a fallacy that behavior with a predominantly genetic origin is necessarily immutable.* The fallacy's underlying assumption is that genetic installations require genetic dis-installations and only learned installations can be unlearned.

The reality is that nature and nurture are inextricably intertwined with the environment doing the selecting in both cases. It does so by conferring survival and reproductive advantage on animals who carry genes "for" certain behaviors and on animals who learn contingencies in real time and use them to advantage. The very capacity to learn is itself genetic.

If an animal is doing it, it's "genetic" (i.e. cows don't climb trees because it's not "genetic"). The only means we have to modify behavior once an animal has been conceived are the tools of operant and classical conditioning, which can affect all behavior. Interestingly, although prognosis in dog-dog aggression is a function of several things, whether the behavior had a mainly genetic installation is not one of them.

So, the "why" behind a given behavior often has little connection to the optimal procedures – well-executed operant and classical conditioning along with careful environmental management – used to modify it once it's up and running.

Dog Social Structure Paradigms

The trickling down of interpretive information extrapolated from the study of captive wolf social behavior has had an overwhelming impact on dog pop psychology. Wolf biologist David Mech refers to this research as "analogous to trying to draw inferences about human family dynamics by studying humans in refugee camps." A wild wolf pack consists of an adult breeding pair and their offspring who have not yet dispersed to form other breeding pairs. Mech is skeptical of historic attempts to view dominance as a temperament trait, pointing out that most wolves, once they disperse from their original familial pack, will breed if they live long enough and once they do, "automatically become alphas."

There is extremely little research on social organization in domestic dogs: a couple of studies on resource competition in dyads, and a bit of research on free-ranging ferals that suggests a rather loose social structure, if any. There have been no credible attempts to suggest how this applies to dogs in the domestic environment, let alone to humans or behavior problems, including aggression. And there has not even been an attempt to link any of models outlined below with increased reproductive success, which in dogs is usually wholly dependent on conformation or on who down the block has a dog of the opposite sex.

This muddled situation has utterly failed to slow down the dog pop psychology machine from interpreting everything from body postures and biting to virtually every behavior problem, as an attempt at ascending in rank. And, not surprisingly, given the absence of inconvenient constraints such as evidence, there is little agreement among proponents of the various proposed hierarchical organizations. I would urge anyone seriously interested in dog social behavior to attend the seminars by the leading dog gurus, write down exactly what they claim about dog social structure and then compare them.

What you will find is that, depending on which dog person is talking, dogs organize themselves into:

- ❑ Strict linear hierarchies, where inferences can be drawn about conflict outcomes for any two animals once the hierarchy is established – dominance is talked about as a relationship between animals rather than as a character trait (i.e. an animal isn't "dominant" per se, but rather is dominant over that one)

- ❑ Non-transitive, or "triangular" hierarchies or parts of hierarchies, where relationships are fixed between any two individuals but cannot be inferred from any

- Contextual dominance relationships where a dog may be dominant over another dog in one context but subordinate to that same dog in another context

- Subordinance hierarchies, as opposed to dominance hierarchies, where the social glue consists of active displays of appeasement of inferiors toward superiors rather than displays of dominance of superiors toward inferiors

- Separate sex systems, for example of the variety where males display linear subordinance (or dominance, depending on who is talking) hierarchies but females display contextual dominance

- Amorphous "tiers" where a character trait determines whether dogs are candidates for the top position or not

- Any of the above with the add-on of "role reversals," where an exchange doesn't play out according to the theory so a temporary role-reversal is invoked to protect the belief system

- Any of the above with the add-on of retention clauses, where an individual can successfully defend a resource once it is in her possession, regardless of the challenger's rank

If you think that's dizzying, consider the following: not one theorist has framed his or her hypothesis into a falsifiable question and then proceeded to go out and test it. What's even more astounding is the way dog people in general have contracted, like a contagious illness, whichever hypothesis appeals to them. They then teach it to the general public as though it were the theory of gravity. The culture is one where anyone can say virtually anything as long as it's compelling sounding and supported by anecdote and the promulgator's belief system. It would be possible to postulate and support virtually any made-up order among a group of dogs given the amount of clauses that can be invoked to protect the theory.

The water is further muddied when one considers that hierarchies imply assumptions about static and equal motivation – that a dog always wants a given resource as much day-to-day, and that any two dogs in a conflict each want the resource equally.

The whole defense of hierarchical models reminds me of epicycles in the geocentric universe. In the 15th century, the earth was presumed to be at the center of the universe and all bodies were presumed to have perfectly circular orbits. As the math became more sophisticated, the movements of planets failed to conform to the theory, so Ptolemy invented epicycles, little extra curlicue motions that the planets made while in orbit, to explain apparent retrograde (backwards) motion in the sky. Of course, the punch line is that – 1400 years later – a more elegant model – that of the sun as center of the solar system etc. won out by explaining much more with fewer assumptions and allowing extremely reliable and precise predictions to be made.

If two dogs fight over a bone and Buffy wins over Reggie, might it be that Reggie learns that he is likely to lose, whereas Buffy learns that competing for the bone pays off? Given any trends in experience, a dog may also generalize and anticipate winning or losing.

It may well be that one of the models put forward for dog social organization is the truth. But this has yet to be established. One important advantage to explanations in learning theory terms is that they open up many doors for intervention: consequences and emotional responses can be altered, thus altering behavior. Social hierarchy models have yielded a history of indirect methods to re-order or reinforce the presumed hierarchy and, worse, they often lead to the use of aversives to "put dogs in their place."

Ever since the publication of *The Culture Clash*, people have asked me whether I "believe in" dominance or pack theory. I'm amazed that questions of this sort, which lend themselves to scientific scrutiny, would ever be a matter of what I or anyone "believes in." Carl Sagan once said, when he was put on the spot about whether he "believed in" the existence of extra-terrestrial visitation that it was not a question of belief but of evidence. After continuing that there was no good evidence that extra-terrestrials had visited, he was pressed with "but what's your gut instinct?" Sagan replied, "I try not to think with my gut."

There are many questions in popular dog psychology that should be a matter of evidence, but seem relegated to the domain of belief. What training procedures work best for what problems and clients? What prevention interventions reduce the incidence of X, Y or Z behavior problems? Do behavior evaluations or "temperament tests" predict any behavior at all subsequent to the test? What is the most accurate model of dog social structure? As long as the level of discussion remains one of beliefs pitted against each other rather than one of objective research, there is likely to be retarded progress on these and other questions.

Most Common Types of Dog-Dog Aggression

When you hear hoof-beats coming over the hill in Wyoming, think horses, not zebras. While it could absolutely be that there are zebras – or albino miniature ponies with pink ribbons in their manes – coming, the first and most obvious thing to rule out is horses.

When it comes to dogs who don't do well with other dogs, there are some common rule-outs that account for the bulk of cases. These are:

- Dogs that come on too strong. They appear hyper-motivated and have coarse social skills. When this type presents along with an impoverished play history, I'm going to refer to them as "Tarzan

- Dogs that are sensitive to the proximity of other dogs. They may present with frank fearfulness or more subtly, as asocial animals that get snappy if a dogs gets too close or makes social overtures

- Dog-dog resource guarding

- Harassment, i.e. bullying or "hazing" of other dogs

- Play skills deficits – dogs that play but lack some of the features of normal play, causing frequent tip-overs of their play into fighting

- Strong genetic predisposition to compulsively fight

This classification system is far simpler than most put forward by dog experts, both bona-fide and self-proclaimed. The types are divided solely by the particular kind of behavior modification techniques used to resolve them. This is why it lumps together kinds of aggression that someone interested in motivational or ethological significance may split apart.

12

Me Tarzan

Dogs are among the most social of species. It would suit them just fine to be around beings they are bonded to 24 hours a day, 7 days a week. They have a repertoire of social signals and, although these are wired genetically, the ease with which they read them in other dogs and the finesse with which they deliver them to other dogs is refined with practice.

There are a great many dogs who lack a sufficiency of experience meeting, greeting and interacting with other dogs. These can present in two ways, either as over-the-top "Tarzans" or as proximity sensitivity. Both of these likely result from the relative social vacuum in which most pet dogs find themselves when they leave their litters. The good news is that this is starting to change: mass owner education combined with more sophisticated and non-aversive training techniques has produced a swell in the number of owners who bring their puppies to puppy classes as well as the quality of these classes. There is even a trend toward earlier puppy classes, where seven to twelve week olds can meet, socialize and commence training. The hygiene measures in early puppy classes must be impeccable, but the early socialization to both dogs and people is well worth the effort.

One of the prime elements in any good puppy class is the allowance of free play. The opportunity to rehearse the reading and expressing of social gestures and the enjoyable time playing – and thus potent positive CER (Conditioned Emotional Response) to other dogs – are invaluable.

Another piece of good news is the establishment of dog parks, areas in public parks where dogs may socialize with each other and play off leash.

The bad news is that, in spite of this increase in puppy classes and dog parks, many, many dogs still have extremely limited experience with members of their own kind once they leave their litters. A swarm of Tarzan type dogs, with a double whammy of extreme over-the-top excitability around other dogs coupled with a poor ability to read and deliver the more subtle versions of dog social signals, is one predictable outcome.

Think of a human who has been raised without being around other people until age 18. Imagine him as a guest at a cocktail party. Not only might he walk on the table and put his fingers in the dip, he might go right up to someone, stand too close, slap them on the back (or worse, grab their privates) and fail to read subtle cues from the host or guests that he is out of line. He is eventually wrestled to the ground and handcuffed. The dog equivalent has terrific interest in other dogs but also lacks social grace.

Here is a typical history of a Tarzan style dog. A puppy is removed from his litter and, because of disease risk, is quarantined away from other dogs until he has been sufficiently vaccinated, which, depending on the vet, may be at around age 3, 4 or 5 months. The owner then starts walking the dog on the street and encountering the occasional dog on leash. The dog's intense excitement, sudden non-responsiveness to the owner and pulling on leash make the owner feel out of control. The concerned owner starts avoiding other dogs, choking up on the leash, jerking the leash or otherwise attempting to discipline the dog, all selectively in the presence of other dogs.

The dog's motivation is increased – partly through deprivation and partly through leash frustration: being rarely able to approach and investigate the other dogs he sees. When he does make contact, his excitement and inexperience cause him to commit social gaffes – he is too much in the other dog's face and fails to read the other dog's body language. Occasional scuffles result. The owner is now more alarmed and escalates the avoidance of dogs, mechanical control procedures as well as the warnings and punishments around other dogs.

The motivation is still off the charts, the skills no better, the dog older and bigger and another element is now added: a growing association of other dogs with frustration, punishment and a tense owner. This grim picture may be further worsened if the dogs he encounters   do not have fantastic social skills either.

This spiral continues until our Tarzan is frankly aggressive to other dogs, often even in other contexts, such as off leash. There are variations on this history and varying degrees of severity, but the combination of limited experience, hyper-motivation, few or no off-leash opportunities, barrier frustration and conditioned association of other dogs with punishment and owner tension are usually present to some degree. This signature history, along with direct observation of meet and greets, is the best way to confirm that this is indeed the problem. It's occasionally possible that Tarzan lives with another dog. While this can attenuate the excitement and language barrier, the skill of meeting, greeting and reading novel dogs may still be coarse.

Proximity Sensitivity

 Not all dogs who lack experience around other dogs become hyper-motivated. Another outcome is social shyness. This can present in a few different ways:

1. Obvious fear and avoidance of other dogs – this is the most easy to spot variation

2. Pro-active lunging, barking and snapping displays that cease once the other dog is far enough away

3. Asocial dogs seemingly disinterested in other dogs until the other dog gets too close or makes social overtures – at this point, threat signals such as growling, snarling, snapping or outright fighting, ensue ("she's fine as long as other dogs don't get in her face")

The histories of proximity sensitive dogs can have common elements with Tarzan histories, most notably no play history, but the problem develops more silently. In the two more subtle variations on this type, the dog, at least early on, seems a model dog when other dogs are around – does not pull on leash, or become agitated in attempting to investigate. Help is sometimes not sought if the owner does not see asocial behavior as a flag. When interaction or proximity with other dogs is forced and aggression results, the owner may be caught completely off guard. The dog may be presented for treatment as "unpredictable," allegedly "fine" with many or most dogs but explosively aggressive with others. What escaped the owner is that the dog was never fine with any dogs, but rather just barely holding it together.

Over time, the pro-active lunging may be acquired through negative reinforcement. The dog learns that displays work to terminate or pre-empt the aversive of dog proximity.

It is important to make a distinction between proximity sensitive dogs and a normal selectiveness, diminished playfulness and decreased tolerance that is developmental in origin. Some dogs will play with any willing dog their entire lives. However, many, starting between ages one and three on average, become more selective about their dog friends, less playful in general and less willing to tolerate crude social behavior from other dogs. The resulting threats and scuffles can result in confusion with the "fine as long as dogs don't get in her face" type of proximity sensitivity.

The differences between the normal development of decreased playfulness, increased selectiveness and decreased tolerance of Tarzan dogs and a dog who is socially shy have to do with onset, history and incidence. If a dog has had limited relationships with other dogs, no play history and is intolerant of virtually all dogs who get too close, it is likely a proximity sensitive dog. Sometimes the history will reveal shyness and avoidance early on and then threat displays later in life, when the dog discovers that these work to keep dogs away.

If, on the other hand, a dog has a history of extensive play and dog relationships and has, in adulthood, started to play less, be more selective and behave aggressively during interactions with certain other dogs who come on strong, it is less likely to be shyness. In these cases, the best course of action is to normalize the dog to the owner so that he doesn't start sequestering or punishing the dog, which could, over the long haul, result in a true deterioration of social skills. Such dogs are valuable players in the social arena, as a matter of fact, provided they have good acquired bite inhibition.

Bullying

Play is apparently highly reinforcing for a great many dogs. The derailing of play by overly rough behaviors therefore serves as a sufficiently rotten consequence to purge it from most dogs' repertoires. Likewise, play attempts directed at non-consenting dogs fall flat and so also usually diminish in frequency. For some dogs, however, roughness and harassment of non-consenting dogs is quite obviously reinforcing. They engage in it at full tilt, with escalating frequency and almost always direct it at designated target dogs. This can be enormously distressing for target dogs, as well as for humans who witness it.

Play Skill Deficits

Sometimes when two dogs are playing, the play becomes too intense and tips over into a fight. The genesis of this can be found in the breakdown, or in severe cases, complete absence, of the role reversals (also called *demeanor shifting*) and constant atmosphere cueing that characterize normal play. When dogs play, there is a frequent give and take: one dog bites the other and then is bitten, one dog chases and then is chased, one dog is on top, then on the bottom. All this is punctuated by continual full or partial play bows, paw raises, inefficient bouncy movements, explosive bluffing-type movements and open,

grinning play faces. When this system breaks down it's as though one dog becomes a broken record, repeating the same thing relentlessly and often with increasing intensity. The other dog's attempts to move on to something else or get his playmate to dial it down a notch are ignored. Irritation, self defense and fighting can ensue.

Certain dogs are prone to tipping over - they don't reverse roles often enough and fail to punctuate their play with atmosphere cues. In contrast to a bully, a dog with a play skill deficit does not direct his ministrations at a specific target dog and, very often, the play starts off normally but then deteriorates. In contrast to a Tarzan type, a dog with a play skill deficit does not improve with carefully orchestrated off-leash socialization. Meet & greets may be normal – the problem emerges as play heats up.

Dog-Dog Resource Guarding

Many beautifully socialized dogs will threaten or bite if approached while eating or while in possession of a coveted object such as bone, pig's ear, their owner, a stick or a stolen piece of laundry. Other dogs may guard sleeping locations such as their bed or get growly when you try to move them off the sofa. This behavior can be directed at humans, at dogs or at both. For information on how to handle resource guarding when it is directed at humans, refer to *Mine! A Guide to Resource Guarding in Dogs*, also in this series.

Dog to dog resource guarding is very common and can crop up in multi-dog households where the dogs are deeply bonded to each other, between dogs who are well acquainted and between perfect strangers. It is an equal opportunity behavior, with virtually all breeds and both sexes represented. Little dogs may successfully guard from larger dogs and less confident dogs may successfully guard from more confident dogs.

In a natural environment, this would be a highly adaptive trait. Magnanimous sharing of scarce resources would not confer advantage on the open plain.   Think of the documentaries you've seen of group living carnivores such as wolves and lions and the incredible acrimony there is around a kill: threat displays, lunging, biting - all first class food guarding.   There has obviously been insufficient artificial selective pressure against this trait in dog breeding programs, as it is so prevalent in domestic dogs who, for the most part, are supplied with an overabundance of food and comfy sleeping locations.

Owners of resource guarders often describe a "Jekyll-Hyde" quality to their dogs.   Their entire demeanor changes once in a guarding context. If the resource is not

19

identified, it can look as though the dog is suddenly being aggressive for no reason. "He's normally so good with Buffy but then suddenly snarled at her and then lunged, without any provocation!"

Compulsive Fighting

Just as dogs can be selectively bred for exaggerated stalking, which translates into herding or pointing, dogs can be bred for increased aggressiveness to other dogs. There are various breeds that have been employed in dog fighting at various points in their history, the most well known of these being the pitbull. Pitbulls were originally bred for a suite of characteristics that made them excel at fighting: a low threshold for dog to dog aggression, "gameness," an uncompromising pugnacity that makes a dog willing to fight on rather than retreating in spite of grievous injury, a characteristic body type, and a failure to  read aggression cut-off switches from other dogs, so that although the other dog may be doing all the right things to inhibit aggression, a pitbull continues to fight.

Interestingly, although the threshold for dog-to-dog aggression was bred low, which makes for a high incidence of fighting, the threshold for aggression directed at humans was bred high in the original stock. What this means is that a game bred dog would be immediately culled if it showed any tendency toward biting people. The reason was to avoid the risk of redirected bites when owners waded into the fray of a dogfight to retrieve their animals.

Pitbulls who have been randomly bred, or bred for other characteristics, such as size (so called "big head" breeding) or, sadly sometimes, aggressiveness to people, may have none, a little, or a lot of the original game-bred characteristics. It's easy to spot some game-bred dogs as

20

they present as extremely scrappy puppies that cannot be left in their own litters for fear of constant fighting. In other cases, the dog presents normally as a puppy and then starts fighting intensely around age two or three, even in spite of competent socialization efforts. It's also important to note that a pitbull without aggression threshold problems might present for dog aggression of another sort, as can any dog.

Multiple Problems

Reality is always a messy business and it is not at all uncommon for a dog to have problems in more than one category. For instance, a dog can be undersocialized and have play skill deficits, or be both a resource guarder and a bully. A compulsive fighter, once rehabbed, may have play-skill deficits that will only become visible once the dog starts playing. In cases where more than one problem is evident, it may be easier to address one of these, managing the other until it is promoted to the front burner. Occasionally it is possible to combine techniques for more than one problem in an all-out assault.

Assessing Prognosis: Acquired Bite Inhibition

By far the most important prognostic factor in dog-dog aggression is the degree of acquired bite inhibition (ABI), which determines how much damage is done when the dog bites. This can range from bites that break bones, deeply puncture muscle and create massive tearing, to bites that leave saliva but no damage whatsoever. There is good predictability in bite severity for the vast majority of dogs once a bite history is known. If, for instance, a dog has had six fights resulting in shallow facial punctures and lacerations or no damage to the other combatant, it's extremely likely subsequent fights will result in a similar range of damage. Although erratic or escalating patterns for bite severity in dog-dog aggression have been documented, and are worrisome from a prognosis standpoint, these are the exception.

The reason ABI is so critical is that the risk of a bite both during and post rehabilitation is huge. When ABI is good, the pace of rehabilitation can be more aggressive and strong reliance on muzzles unnecessary. Subsequent to rehab, there is assurance that any normal squabbling throughout the dog's life will be without serious ramification. By contrast, a dog with poor ABI must be managed much more carefully throughout rehab. And, even if the presenting problem is beautifully resolved, the likelihood of any individual dog making it to the end of his life without ever having one altercation with another dog is low. And, with prior knowledge that any such altercation will result in serious injury, there is some strong moral and legal imperative to manage tightly forever more.

To assess ABI, there is no better means than Ian Dunbar's bite/fight ratio. Divide the number of trips to the veterinarian (for the opponent of the dog in question) for suturing of wounds by the number of fights. This is an objective measure, far better than eyeballing fights. There  is zero correlation between how ugly or intense looking a dogfight is and the degree of damage done. In fact, given the forms of ritualization dogs employ, it is likely that the more dramatic, noisy, snarly fights will have the least serious damage.

One important caveat is that there is not perfect agreement among veterinarians with regard to what kinds of wounds require shaving, suturing and antibiotics and what kinds do not. For this reason, it is not a perfectly objective barometer. A measurement of puncture depth would be better but is usually not available. Dog variables also make a difference. A bite of identical pressure delivered to the neck scruff of a Siberian and the shoulder of a whippet might cause very different degrees of damage. For this reason, always take into consideration the presence of taut skin and sparse coat, which facilitate puncturing.

When interviewing the client to assess ABI, maintain focus on the *number* of fights and *number* of serious injuries. Note the word *number*. Clients are often keen to convey interpretive information to you such as the dog's presumed thoughts, motives and intentions as well as those of his opponent. While a thorough client interview will gather all relevant information, in the course of bite inhibition assessment, stick to the bite/fight numbers. How many fights has the dog had? How many dogs of which breeds were injured on what parts of their bodies and with what degree of damage?

Sometimes the bite inhibition history is paltry or non-existent. The dog may have had some fights but the owner is unsure about the degree of damage done. Or, the dog is growly and lungy but has never had a fight. In such cases, an idea about the degree of acquired bite inhibition can be obtained by taking note of any bite history with humans, the dog's adult contact play history with other dogs, if any, the dog's bite inhibition when play-biting humans, if he does so and, finally, the dog's gentleness when being hand-fed. An adult contact play history is that of a dog who, as an adult, regularly plays with other dogs and, when doing so, mouths and jaw-wrestles with them. The jury would be out, in other words, on a dog who plays but does so without ever putting his mouth on the other dog (e.g. only chases, paws, is himself mouthed etc.).

These indicators are inferior to a fight history. The greatest possible confidence level about what degree of damage a dog will inflict when he is next going to be in a dogfight is the degree of damage he has inflicted in the past in that same context. My recommendation for dogs with unknown ABI is to employ a muzzle any time the dog is worked in proximity to other dogs, unless evidence emerges that the

ABI is good. It would also be prudent to screen such a dog carefully for aggression directed at people, as many believe there may be a relationship between ABI in dog-dog cases and ABI in dog-people cases.

Assessing Prognosis: Other Factors

Bite inhibition is the most important factor to consider when assessing prognosis. The other factors that come into play for dog-dog problems are:

- ❑ Owner commitment and compliance

- ❑ Bite threshold and presence of protracted warning

- ❑ Dog learning rate

- ❑ Available recruitment pool

Client Compliance

Client compliance is a key limiting factor in the success of any behavior modification program, and dog-dog aggression is no exception. An otherwise good prognosis coupled with a competent trainer, sound procedure and good coaching is for naught if the owner cannot follow instructions, abide by management rules, and stick with the program.

Bite Threshold and Protracted Warning

Bite inhibition and bite threshold are often confused. Where bite inhibition refers to the amount of pressure exerted when the dog does bite, bite threshold refers to the number and intensity of trigger(s) required to get the dog to bite. This comes into play most often with proximity sensitive dogs. When another dog gets close enough to elicit a reaction, proximity sensitive dog A might freeze, give a hard stare and then, as the dog gets closer and closer, growl, snarl and then lunge snapping and barking if the dog gets right on top of him. Proximity sensitive dog B might, as soon as the other dog gets close enough to make him uncomfortable, lunge and bite. Dog A would be described as having a high bite threshold with many protracted warnings – all that growling, snarling and snapping is a big advertisement to stay away – whereas dog B would be described as having a low bite threshold with no protracted warning. Although the two often go together, it's also possible to have the presence of lots of threat signals together with a relatively low bite threshold. It is always less risky to treat dogs who have high bite thresholds and who give protracted warnings when their buttons start to be pushed.

(Hmm...what the hell is that? If it comes closer I will bite it)

GRRR!!!! YAP-AP-AP-AP-AP-AP!!!! What the HELL is that?!?!

Learning Rate

Dogs differ in a myriad of ways and one of these is the ease and speed with which they can be conditioned. Some dogs seem to progress rapidly at all kinds of learning tasks, and others seem to have specific aptitudes. It is not known whether these differences are primarily due to genetics, experience or both. One effect that is well known, however, is that of the learning to learn effect. Contrary to the myth that puppies or younger dogs are easier to train, dogs who have learned things before are usually easier to train due to this previous experience.

Occasionally, training histories can be obstacles, as when a dog with a long history of being trained with aversives is first free-shaped with a clicker. The dog's repertoire has been so truncated by chronic punishment that there may be initial unwillingness of offer behaviors. This effect is also sometimes seen to a lesser degree in dogs who have histories of being prompted a great deal and then are free-shaped.

In the case of dog-dog aggression rehab, a prior learning history or an overall facility with learning might provide a head start for a particular intervention (and even influence your decision to use a particular tool, like a clicker).

Recruiting

An important limiting factor when working on any kind of aggression problem is the availability of individuals in the stimulus category you're working on. Although it is possible to make gains by working opportunistically, i.e. by exploiting those chance encounters with people or dogs that occur in everyday life, the degree of control over stimulus intensity is usually poor. This not only may slow progress down but can even be counterproductive. Also, there is usually not the chance for multiple trials in succession, and the number of trials may be too small to make any significant progress.

For these reasons, having a pool of people or dogs to recruit for training sessions is invaluable. In the case of dog-dog aggression problems, this vital recruiting can be constrained by both availability and willingness. There simply may not be suitable dogs around or if there are, the owners may not be willing to subject them to the presence of a dog that may threaten, harass or attack them.

There are two genuine risks to the dogs used in training exercises or remedial socialization: 1) physical damage should the dog bite them badly, and 2) an aversive experience resulting in fear conditioning even in the absence of a damaging bite. Although these risks are always minimized and, in the hands of a competent practitioner, harm is almost never done to recruited dogs, the perceptions owners have of the process can temper the willingness of many people to lend their dogs to the cause. The steps needed to minimize risk will be laid out in the sections on techniques. For now, it's important just to be aware of the how the absence of recruitment options can limit prognosis.

Resolving Tarzan Style Aggression

Aggression as a result of apparent hyper-motivation and coarse social skills may be presented as on or off leash aggression of varying severity. The hallmark in the history is the sequestering of the dog relatively early on by an alarmed owner who studiously avoids other dogs, with little or no play preceding this strategy. If this type of dog is presented early enough, there may not be frank aggression at all – the dog may simply be ultra excited and coarse during meet and greets, and never has off-leash opportunities.

Another flag in the history is heavy use of mechanical control around other dogs, i.e. an extremely tight, shortened leash. The owner's mis-handling is perfectly understandable, by the way, given the cavernous void of good information on dog behavior and training that exists in the popular press.

The best outcome, for Tarzan type dogs with good acquired bite inhibition, is achieved using a combination of:

1) Remedial off-leash socialization with carefully selected dogs and

2) Operantly conditioning better manners for on-leash encounters.

The remedial socialization greatly facilitates the on-leash manners work and for this reason should be commenced first. Not only does it start to dent the hyper-motivation and polish up the social skills, it provides some reassurance to the owner that their dog is not trying to kill other dogs. This then allows the owner to relax and learn how to handle the on-leash meet & greets with greater finesse.

Bite Inhibition Caveat

In my opinion, under no circumstances should a dog with poor bite inhibition – a dog that has a pattern of causing injuries to other dogs during fights – be considered a candidate for remedial off-leash socialization. The likelihood of re-offense during or post rehab is too great. In fact, even among those with no identified problem, it is a rare dog that engages in regular off-leash interaction and never, ever has an argument with another dog.

The one exception would be a dog with poor bite inhibition that always wears a properly fitted basket muzzle. This can allow for some ability to socialize. One potential obstacle is the stigma of muzzles resulting in poor treatment of the dog's owner by an intolerant dog park culture when the dog becomes dog park ready.

Dog Selection for Remedial Socialization

It is extremely important to screen the dogs used for remedial socialization with great care. They should be *extensively* socialized – at the upper end of the continuum in terms of number of novel social contacts in adulthood. A dog who has a dog friend or two is not what I'm talking about, but rather dog park junkies who meet and greet scores of dogs every week. They have played with countless of these dogs. They have encountered all manner of behavior and personality. They read and deliver body language effortlessly. They have had fights and dusted themselves off without issue. They are the "professionals" of the doggy interaction world. Dog trainers refer to them as "bullet-proof" or "bomb-proof."

The reason one needs bulletproof dogs for remedial socialization is that, although there is minimal injury risk if the bite inhibition is good, the risk of a recruited dog being psychologically damaged is high if he is not sufficiently "padded." A severe Tarzan can dish out some pretty awful stuff and this could result in undesired conditioning in an unpadded dog. Imagine if a young dog, Melba, has met two or three dogs with some success and then is subjected to a Tarzan racing up, body-slamming, growling, mounting and failing to turn any of this off when Melba delivers "back off" body language. Melba may very well end up with a fearful emotional response to not only our Tarzan but to dogs that remind her of him, to most large dogs except those in her circle already or, in the worst case, to all dogs.

So, the greater the number of successful social contacts, the better the padding. For each dog, the critical mass of padding to render him or her bulletproof may differ significantly. Some dogs cope just fine with fights or coarse treatment by other dogs relatively early on in their careers, without any generalization to other dogs or effect on their demeanors, whereas other dogs seem prone to developing outright phobias if their experience has not been overwhelmingly positive for an extensive period. The prudent course of action when recruiting is to select only those dogs that have extensive socialization histories including evidence of bounce-back from bad experiences.

Another reason to go for slick, playful dogs is that they will have the best chance of eliciting better behavior in the target dog. I suggest having three or four other dogs in the playgroup early on when doing remedial socialization as this best "dilutes" Tarzan. If only one or two dogs are available, however, you may still proceed. It's also ideal if these dogs are not significantly smaller than Tarzan.

Prep Work for Remedial Socialization

In order for Tarzan to learn the social ropes, release him off leash in a well-secured area with the chosen bulletproof "therapist" dogs. The area should be large enough to allow dogs ample choice of position and distance but not so large that a dogfight could take place too far away to allow for relatively quick pull-aparts. Having the area be secure – fenced or a large, closed room with good footing – ensures unintended dogs don't wander in as well as keeping the playgroup from getting out.

There should be at least two experienced people present. Also, if there are more than two dogs participating, there must be at least one person per dog. If two dogs start
30

fighting, the most experienced people will break up the fight (if necessary) while others secure the other dogs present so that they do not gravitate toward the fight.

Stock a fight kit for use during off-leash dog-dog rehab. In it should be metal pots or stainless steel water dishes, two pairs of animal control gloves, a break stick, citronella spray and pepper spray.

Breaking Up Dog Fights

There is no golden standard for breaking up a dogfight, but there are as many opinions as there are dog owners. My recommendation is to try a sudden aversive, such as a loud noise near the combatants as a first line of defense. Bang the pots and pans or steel water dishes together while yelling. Cease the instant the dogs disengage.

If this doesn't work (try for two or three seconds, then move on), the two most experienced people, wearing the animal control gloves, will each pull one dog off as follows:

1) Grip the base of the tail where it joins the body

2) Pull both dogs simultaneously quickly out and up, raising the rear quarters of the ground

Secure both dogs with leashes and assess for damage.

If the dog has no tail, grasp the dog's rear legs close to the dog's groin to pull him off. Never pull a dog by the rear leg by grasping under the knee joint, as the risk of knee injury is substantial.

If this doesn't work, use the citronella and, if that doesn't work, the pepper spray. Other people present should be securing all dogs not involved in the fight.

The very last resort to consider is pulling dogs out by their collars or necks. This is because of the significant risk of an accidental or re-directed bite. This risk is even greater if you are without gloves, which offer some protection. Many of the worst bites are sustained putting hands into fights.

If ever you find yourself breaking up a dogfight by yourself, try first noise, then citronella or pepper spray. If you are empty-handed, pull the more intense fighter off yourself. If you can't tell which is the more intense fighter, go for the dog you are less likely to be able to control with your voice. Usually this means, if one of the dogs is your own, pulling the other dog off.

Breaking up a fight on your own is an extremely unpleasant jam to be caught in. Most people still feel, however, that if the fight looks grave enough, they will risk it to help their dog.

Latch-Ons

Latch-ons occur when one dog gets a hold of another and will not let go. They are alarming for people to witness, however are usually not as serious as they look.

First assess whether the dog being bitten is losing consciousness or is panicking – this will determine how you will subsequently proceed. If the dog is awake and alert and not panicking, wait it out – hold the latching dog by the collar and try to distract him by talking to him, bribing him, getting him in a better frame of mind. Do not attempt to pull the other dog out of his mouth as this can cause tearing injuries as well as amping up the latching dog. Once the latched dog disengages, get him out of range and assess the bitten dog.

If the dog being latched onto is losing consciousness or is panicking, it is an emergency. If you have a fight kit, straddle the latching dog, grab his collar with one hand and, with the other, insert the break stick into the gap at the corner of his mouth. Break sticks are wedge shaped and designed for this very purpose. Rotate the break stick (as though revving the throttle of a motorcycle). As soon as the jaws open, haul the latching dog off.

When the latch-on is desperate and no break stick available, the last resort measures I have heard include collar twists to cut off the latching dog's airway and elicit mouth-opening to breath, attempts to pry jaws open with hands, testicle grabbing, eye-gouging, inserting something into the latching dog's rectum, kicking and attempts to get the dog re-latched onto an article of clothing or one's arm. Fortunately, latch-ons are relatively rare events outside the dog-fighting culture.

Running a Tarzan Therapy Group

Once you've got the dogs, the seasoned dog people, the space and a fight kit, you're ready to start the play group. Release all dogs simultaneously without any fanfare. Tarzan will likely beeline for the nearest dog and work his magic. Monitor closely in case of a fight; however refrain from intervening during any strong posturing and "snarking" (snarly "back off" barking lunges).

Tarzan will take some lumps for the rude and crude behavior. The rude and crude stuff will go down in frequency and he will then be paid off for more circumspect and respectful interactions by being played with. It's a fascinating process to watch. He may appear mainly interested in strutting stiffly around looking for some four-legged to mount or stand over. Play will likely break out among the socialized dogs and this ought to have a seductive effect sooner or later.

Fighting with Absence of Play

Our hope is that Tarzan will do some playing in that very first session, usually after being ignored for the stiff and growlies and perhaps being blasted a few times for coming on too strong. If fighting breaks out – as it often will early  on in the session – break it up, let the dogs cool down for thirty seconds or so and then let them go again. The instinct of many dog owners is to get the fighting dogs into separate counties as quickly as possible. In fights stemming from rude, naïve behavior, however, the lowest likelihood of fighting tends to be immediately after a fight. The fight is apparently a self-punishing event. Contrast this with bullies, dogs with play-skill deficits or compulsive fighters, in whom fights appear to not be punishing events at all and may even be reinforcing.

If outright fighting continues for more than two or three rounds, take a longer break to evaluate what's happening and allow the dogs to regroup. The main objective at this point is to ascertain whether the problem really is hyper-motivation and coarse social skills. The possibilities are three:

1) There is another problem instead of or in addition to the socialization deficit – the possible suspects are severe proximity sensitivity, bullying, inter-male and compulsive fighting

2) The problem is truly impoverished socialization but the particular group chemistry is unfavorable

3) The problem is truly impoverished socialization but in its most severe form – the dog is in a deep rut

To start thinking in an organized way about what's going on, the first factor is whether the group is composed of one dog besides the target Tarzan or two or more besides the target dog. If there is just one other dog present, it's more difficult to feel confident about interpreting the fights. The most valuable course of action in this case is to try Tarzan in a group of two or three other dogs. To help rule inter-male in or out, have both sexes present if the original group consisted of a male Tarzan and one other male.

If there are no other dogs to recruit – this is a distinct possibility since if there were, you likely would have used them in the first place – your choices are to a) put Tarzan on a muzzle and long line to rein him in – in other words, treat him as a chronic fighter, regardless of what he actually is, and continue to work with the dog you do have; b) hope he's a severe Tarzan and try the same thing one more time on another day, after an intense aerobic exercise session for Tarzan; or c) work him as an on-leash only case unless other bullet-proof dogs crop up.

The most important thing is to not continue to subject even a bullet-proof dog to a dog who may very well have some other type of problem that is not appropriate for remedial socialization or the continual attack of a very severe Tarzan type without any other dogs to share the load.

If there were two or more dogs and Tarzan kept attacking one of them, first note whether he ignored the other dog by default (too busy attacking dog A to notice dog B at all) or whether there was any semblance of social behavior directed at one dog but repeated fights at every opportunity with the other. In the latter case, there could be a chemistry issue between the two fighters. Another possibility is inter-male aggression if Tarzan and his opponent were both male and there was some greeting or investigation but no aggression with any female(s) present. The final remote possibility is bullying.

 If Tarzan was so busy attacking one dog that the jury was out on his disposition toward the other(s), try removing the opponent to see if he proceeds to fight with those remaining or does anything else. Again, consider the sex differences to see if inter-male aggression can be ruled out. If the clear trend is that greeting and investigation, however crude, are directed at females and very little at males along with chronic fighting with males, this begins to look like inter-male aggression along with the impoverished socialization. Do remedial play groups with females and then proceed with a regular inter-male (i.e. resource guarding) protocol.

If he is more sociable, even crudely, with other dogs aside from the target dog, it could be simply a chemistry mis-match or, again, less likely, bullying. Bullying is usually characterized by gradual onset though it's possible that right from puppyhood, a bully is born and blossoms and then is sequestered, which adds a layer of hypermotivation on the original problem.

A chemistry mis-match simply means the dogs didn't like each other, for any one of a number of reasons, and fought. In the case of a Tarzan, there are many shades of what not to like and not every bulletproof dog will defuse every Tarzan, or punish successfully or efficiently. There are as many opinions about exactly what the dynamic is in this situation as there are dog trainers and I don't want to speculate any further. The solution is to omit that dog from early playgroups, and try re-incorporating him or her later, when Tarzan has improved.

How Many Play Sessions and How Often?

With Tarzan type dogs, the more play sessions with bulletproof dogs, the better. Each play session should go to the point of boredom, i.e. the dogs have moved onto investigating other things or simply hanging out in the play area, rather than intensely interacting. This is the opposite strategy to what many trainers use in routine dog training, where the idea is to leave the dog wanting more at the end of a training session to help maintain motivator value and the dog's keenness. In remedial socialization, the more the motivator – the other dog – becomes saturated, the better. A large part of the problem here is hyper-motivation, a problem many trainers would dearly love to have for the motivators they can more easily control.

To reach the boredom point most efficiently, as well as to keep the level of difficulty as low as possible, re-use the same playgroup many times. This also helps the initial off-leash meet and greet, where most of Tarzan's fireworks are confined, by exploiting the "oh you again" effect. When Tarzan seems slicker with this group, it's time to rotate new bulletproof dogs in. You can tell Tarzan is slicker by:

- ❑ More polished meet and greets – Tarzan pulls himself up wagging and

- ❏ Fewer fights per unit time, and

- ❏ High volume of consenting play

The old bulletproof crew is still valuable – they should be present to dilute newcomers. Also, you can squeeze some extra usefulness out of them by employing them for cold trial meet and greets in locations apart from the playgroup area.

It's extremely good practice to keep detailed track of whether there is improvement or not, rather than relying on your or the owner's subjective impressions. If all bodies on hand are needed for fight protocol implementation, one way to allow data recording is to videotape the session for later review. Note the total off-leash interaction time, number of fights, when in the session they occurred, their duration, whether they spontaneously resolved or had to be broken up, the means of breaking up each fight if applicable, which dogs were involved, post-fight demeanor of Tarzan and when play commenced as well as qualitative descriptions of any play, and when play wound down and boredom set in.

The overall trend we're after is reduced fights, shorter fights that are easier to break up and play beginning earlier in the session. An important word about overall trends. Beware of putting too much emphasis on magnified local trends. For instance, if, in play session number five, there is a knock-down brawl that is very hard to break up and that happens to be followed by reduced play, don't panic about trend if the overall pattern from sessions one through eight is in the right direction. If you flip a coin fifty times, the trend will lean toward 50-50 heads to tails but there may be a string of four or five heads in a row at some point. This is not necessarily evidence of anything supernatural. In behavior, we're almost always more interested in trends than in short strings that wash out probability wise when you zoom out and see the big picture.

When to Expose Tarzan to Regular Dogs

The ideal is to keep rotating novel bulletproof dogs through the therapy group until Tarzan demonstrates polished meet and greets, even cold with novel dogs, and the sessions are virtually fight-free. You may, however, exhaust the bulletproof dog supply before you reach absolute perfection. If this is the case, carry on with what you've got and introduce the first non-bullet-proof dog at the end of a play session. Between the warm-up, physical fatigue and dilution in the group, the chances of mishap are minimized. This hierarchy formula of balancing novelty against degree of warm-up and physical fatigue is a good one to be familiar with.

When Tarzan has logged a significant number of nice looking play hours with three or more dogs, including reasonable meet and greets, I would submit that he's dog park ready. Dog park composition is, of course, less controlled. But the cost-benefit analysis is overwhelming. Dogs like this stand to benefit so enormously from regular exposure and slide downhill when sequestered. A good way to segue into the dog park is to meet one of his regular buddies there at a low-density time. There is then some chance that he will get some warm up with the familiar dog before having to meet and greet an unknown quantity.

Part of the challenge of throwing Tarzan into the deep end is owner reticence. It's worth talking them through the worst-case scenario. A partially rehabbed dog with some clear motivation to play, some budding play skills and a known good mouth is neither morally nor legally questionable. There may be a squabble and some mildly upset owners. Most owners who attend dog parks know this activity presumes some risk. A good many people with completely unknown quantities – adult dogs with years of yard-only exercise, newly rescued adults, adolescents that have been quarantined etc. – routinely toss them into the mix at dog parks and most learn to swim.

If Tarzan keeps does not begin playing at the park, sit down and analyze why. Presuming some improvement in the therapy groups, the possible explanations are:

1) Extra problem nested inside the socialization deficit – bullying, play skill problems, inter-male or compulsive fighting

2) Consistently poor group chemistry

3) Sensitization – Tarzan meets up with a problematic dog early on, gets amped up and this colors his subsequent interactions, even those with more normal dogs

Regardless of what is going on, arrange a "recovery" therapy group with known successful playmates before trying the park again. If you are leaning toward thinking there may be other problems, carry on the therapy groups and tackle the other problem using the instructions in this manual. If you suspect bad luck with the group chemistry, scope out the dog park before entering (Tarzan will do poorly with proximity sensitive dogs and certainly could be targeted by a bully or an adult male, especially if Tarzan is an adolescent or young adult). If you suspect sensitization, arrange for one of his known buddies to be there to meet him and be first playmate. If you're really unsure what's going on, it's worth trying again and having an extra person on hand so you can pay close attention and/or videotape.

Other Tarzan Combinations

As I mentioned earlier on, dogs may end up sequestered at a young age secondary to bullying as a puppy. The same thing can happen with resource (often owner) guarding that blooms early, and with severe play skill deficits. Sequestering then results in impoverished overall socialization and possible Tarzan features on top of the original problem. The chance of other nested problems should not deter you from commencing the Tarzan part when this is present. It may, however, be prudent, depending on the severity of the other suspected issue, to use bulletproof dogs until the additional issue is discovered and resolved. In many cases, these will not surface until the dog has been worked on enough to allow for normal play.

In the case of a mild or extremely intermittent problem - resource guarding can present this way -, it may be possible to manage while overall social skills develop. These in turn, may aid the eventual resource guarding work, or even render it unnecessary.

On-Leash Manners Training for Tarzan

In the case of undersocialized and hyper-motivated dogs where acquired bite inhibition is poor, the option of remedial socialization is, in my opinion, prohibitively risky. As I mentioned earlier in the book, even if the dog can be gotten to play normally with other dogs, the knowledge that if and when the dog ever has a routine scuffle with another dog, there will be serious injuries, has enormous moral and legal implications. For this reason, when the bite inhibition is poor, you will put all your modification eggs into the basket of on-leash meet and greet training. Remedial socialization on muzzle is still a viable option, as long as the muzzle is not dispensed with once the dog's social skills are normal.

Undersocialized dogs with good bite inhibition will also usually need on-leash manners training even if the remedial socialization goes swimmingly. Consider it a bonus if the remedial socialization so dampens hyper-motivation in on-leash meet & greets that no formal exercises are necessary. The on-leash work can commence once the remedial socialization is well underway (3+ sessions in). It is inefficient to do this prior to commencing remedial socialization because the dog is easier to work on leash once the off-leash social skills are starting to develop and the hyper-motivation dented. Also, the owner has seen the dog interact with and not kill other dogs, which is good for the cause. And, given the leash handling ability of most people, I do think it is easier for dogs to learn develop nuances at giving and receiving body language off leash than on.

The two exercises for on-leash manners training are:

1) Loose-leash approach training

2) Leash handling during mutual investigations

Use of Halters

The exercise is greatly facilitated by the dog wearing a head halter, such as a Gentle Leader or Snoot Loop. If the dog has never worn one before, it's inadvisable to put one on for the first time to do dog approach exercises. Pre-install it first. You can desensitize him gradually as per the instructions below, or put it on for normal walks and see if he habituates. Many dogs will fight a halter pretty strenuously the first few walks but then begin to ignore it and soon after, happily anticipate the walk it predicts.

If you choose to go the habituation route, offer to handle for the owner the first time out. Ignore the dog's attempts to paw or otherwise remove the halter and praise and feed him for walking. Keep the leash loose except when the dog lowers his head to facilitate vigorous pawing or scraping and slithering along the ground. Gently lift his head with the leash and remove this pressure once he stops trying to paw and/or lower his head to the ground.

There's no question that slapping a halter on many dogs is aversive. If this kind of aversive is more than you're willing to utilize or if, even after being briefed by you about what to expect, the handler is too distressed seeing the dog struggle and fuss with the halter, it's probably better to go the desensitization route. You may also decide to switch to desensitization if the dog doesn't improve on the halter over the course of the first couple of walks. Once the dog has accepted the halter, use it for the dog approach exercises.

Head Halter Desensitization

Progress to the next step only when you have achieved the goal on the current step. You can expect to spend a few days completing all the steps if you work at least once a day for 15-20 minutes.

1. Show the dog the halter and then give him a generous handful of tasty treats – repeat this several times with long pauses in between until he is demonstrating a happy, anticipatory response whenever you make it visible. In between trials, hang out with him without feeding him and with the halter hidden.

2. Teach the dog to target the halter by rewarding him every time he bumps it with his nose. A clicker is invaluable here to mark good responses with precision timing. For information on clicker

training, see Karen Pryor's wonderful book *Don't Shoot the Dog!*

3. When the dog is nose targeting over and over, wait for two or three bumps per reward. While doing so, try to select the nose bumps that are a little longer and stronger.

4. Hold the halter up with the correctly sized nose loop open and lure the dog's muzzle through with a treat. Do this several times and then hold off on the lure and wait for the dog to put his nose in or near the loop by himself. The goal is better and better approximations of putting his nose all the way in on his own.

5. When he puts his nose into the halter, wait a second or so before rewarding. After several rewards for one-second duration, go to two and then three seconds. Praise him while he's in the loop. Gradually increase the time he must remain in to 10 seconds.

6. Adjust the halter's head strap so that it would fit him extremely loosely were it on. Now, while he is waiting in the nose loop for his treat, snap the loose head strap on, treat and then remove the halter. Repeat and add some duration to the loosely fitted halter wearing.

7. Adjust the head strap so that it is closer and closer to a correct fit (for a Gentle Leader, this is extremely snugly around the back of his head, high up under the occiput, the pointy bone there). Once the halter is at the correct fit, gradually add duration until he is wearing the properly fitted halter for 10 seconds.

8. Take normal walks with the halter, feeding often and ignoring any minor fussing.

Client Mentoring

If you're a trainer working with a client, you will handle the dog for the first session, and possibly more, narrating for the client what you are doing. The next step will be the client handling while you prompt and reinforce their actions. Only when you find the client is requiring no prompting from you to handle correctly will you let the client practice without you present. This is a good protocol to follow for all types of client executed training.

Some dog trainers are reluctant to offer this degree of supervision, feeling guilty about "taking the client's money." In no other endeavor, however, where someone had to master as complex a set of mechanical skills as is needed to leash handle a difficult dog effectively, would any teacher do anything but monitor closely. Imagine piano teachers, scuba diving instructors, speech pathologists or driving instructors simply demonstrating or explaining and then abandoning students to flounder on their own.

You'll also need an accomplice to handle the other dog. They needn't be an expert dog handler, just someone to hold the leash of the other dog. The other dog should be socialized – neither a Tarzan nor fearful type. If there is absolutely nothing else available, it's possible to make some headway with a poorly socialized other dog in the early stages of the exercise, where the target Tarzan learns he can gain ground by keeping the leash loose and following simple instructions such as sit. To get to the actual meet and greet, however, the other dog must be sufficiently socialized to be able to withstand what may be a crude greeting and to not make things worse with his or her own unpolished behavior.

It of course adds logistical set-up energy to recruit the other handler and dog for the session but it is infinitely more productive to do it this way than to take one's chances on a real walk. One might encounter other Tarzans, bona fide aggressive dogs, poorly handled dogs, dogs who will be traumatized by Tarzan, loose dogs or no dogs. Good dog training means setting the dog up to make gains, not gambling and then wasting time or possibly doing harm.

Basic Meet & Greets

A good meet and greet consists of the two dogs smoothly making muzzle to muzzle contact followed by some mutual rear investigation. Then either play will break out or the dogs will go their separate ways. A male may urinate on the next available vertical surface.

Meet and greets may feature stiffness, posturing and snarky stuff. The latter sometimes indicates some lack of social skill or confidence, or simply routine friction in normal dog interactions.

It's a good general policy with unknown quantity dogs to break meet & greets off after several seconds, if the dogs don't do so themselves. I recommend allowing posturing, stiffness or standing over, provided there is rapid enough behavior change, i.e. the dogs don't get stuck in some volatile looking stance such as a stiff and growly T-position (perpendicular to each other with one dog's chin or chest over withers of other). If there is some snarking or if they get stuck in some stiff posture, break them off. Happy talk them while walking away if one or both dogs are too stiff.

If you want to try again after breaking it off, wait a couple of minutes before re-engaging to let them cool off. Keep the dogs moving during the break and keep up the happy talk even as you disengage. Put the problem dog(s) through some obedience paces at some distance. Then try again. This is not the same advice as for routine off-leash scuffles, where re-engagement is immediate.

In the case of a dog with a known impoverished socialization history and perhaps some frank aggression, the goal is to normalize meet and greets. To accomplish this, Tarzan must have mastered basic loose-leash walking in situations without dogs present and the owner must first learn how to handle during a meet and greet. Let's look at these two components first.

Loose Leash Walking Exercises

Practice with no other dogs around at first. This is an appropriate level of difficulty for both dog and owner. If the dog has already had successful loose leash training, skip this part and go right ahead to the meet and greet practice.

The first objective is for the owner to grasp that the reinforcer for the dog is progress in the direction the dog would like to go. This now must become precisely contingent on whether the leash is loose or tight. This is one of those things that is extremely obvious to dog trainers but much, much less so to non-trainers. Invite the owner to focus on the leash and first notice whether it's loose or tight. Then narrate the exercise, all the minute decisions you make regarding stopping and starting and how you are completely focused on the looseness of the leash.

Point out that you're holding the leash with both hands on the same point and that the leash is close to your body.

This improves control, especially if the dog is on a regular flat collar as opposed to a head halter, and provides a consistent length of leash between handler and dog, making it easier for the dog to learn the distance from the handler that makes the brakes go on, and thus anticipate it and avoid more punishers (cessation of progress forward).

This technique, coined "red light green light" by Ian Dunbar, requires some resolve and timing but is well worth the effort. If you've not done it much, here are some pointers.

Stand absolutely still and wait for the dog to slacken the leash before praising and moving forward. The first several times will be by pure chance. Sometimes it helps to place a moderately valuable "goal," such as a small pile of cookies, a short distance away, especially if the training is in a familiar place where the dog may not necessarily be inclined to pull anyway, or may collect rewards in the form of novel smells for sniffing here or there even if the technique is diligently applied.

There are different schools of thought when it comes to the question of whether to prompt the dog for some early successes or wait him out. No one really knows which is faster in the long run for the majority of dogs – it remains in the realm of opinion, so feel free to train however you – or the client – are most comfortable.

However it's attained – by prompting or waiting – as soon as there's slack on the leash, praise and take a step in the direction the dog was straining. The dog will likely surge forward. This is your cue to stop and start waiting again. You can mark the boo-boo with a no-reward-mark (NRM – a conditioned negative punisher) such as "too bad" or not. The advantage of any conditioned reinforcer or punisher is in improved timing, so if you suspect your timing is less than stellar, go ahead and bridge.

I have had some good success with doling out one or two yard penalties for pulling. Rather than simply putting the brakes on, actually take a couple of steps backward away from the direction the dog has chosen. This increases the cost to the dog of pulling by making it much worse for him. It also conditions the NRM more quickly if, after each NRM, the dog is hauled back further from his goal. This in turn speeds no-pull conditioning if the NRM is being used.

How long it takes to teach a dog to walk on a loose leash varies wildly and probably is a factor of the learning rate and impulsivity of the dog, timing of the handler and consistency of training. As I said, it's well worth persevering, both for the lifetime of better leash manners and for the contribution this exercise makes to overall impulse control. The more dogs are taught things like stay, wait at doorways, leave it or don't touch, anti-jump exercises and anti-pull exercises, the better ingrained the general principle of "don't be a bull in the china shop when you want something – good things come to those who wait," something most dog owners find extremely likeable.

To protect the behavior when the owner takes the dog out in day to day life and needs to move from A to B and hence may end up rewarding pulling, cue the contingency from the first training session. This is contrary to most shaping endeavors, where behavior is not put on cue until all parameters have been added and the behavior strong and in its final form. So, whenever "don't pull please" or whatever command will be used is given, it signals that the red light green light rules are on. Ideally, the dog will only be taken out on leash this way but if not, the cue may help prevent confusion and weakening of behavior.

Once the dog has some competence at keeping the leash loose without dogs around, it's time to practice meet and greets, first with normal dogs to rehearse the owner's handling, and then on Tarzan.

On Leash Meet and Greet Handling Practice

The following exercise focuses on achieving deft leash-handling and improving decision making about when to force a break-off – which can function as both a negative punisher and a management tool.

This is very much about good handling so practice first with two normal dogs so the owner can become fluent with the leash handling. Demonstrate walking up, red light green light style, keeping the leash loose as the dogs meet muzzle to muzzle (handler's job to keep leash loose here, not dog's), keeping up a steady stream of happy talk and then the handlers following their dogs smoothly around during a circle investigation to avoid tangled leashes. Narrate it a couple of times and then coach the owner through handling one of the dogs. A key skill is that of being bubbly, loose and happy on the outside but vigilant and planning for emergency break-aways on the inside. This ability to maintain high situational alertness without any telegraphing of tension to the dog takes some rehearsal and confidence.

When the owner is comfortable and error-free with normal meet and greets, commence the training exercises with Tarzan.

On Leash Meet and Greets with Tarzan

This is a DRI (differential reinforcement of incompatible behavior, or operant counterconditioning) exercise. The dog learns that keeping the leash loose pays off whereas tightening the leash does not. The pay-offs are 1) continued approach toward the other dog, 2) tasty treats and 3) enthusiastic praise. Before commencing these exercises, the dog should have had some basic anti-pull training around other types of distractions and be fluent at these.

The choice of motivator will fluctuate depending on what the dog indicates he is most into on any given trial. It's always important to identify the "gold medal" motivator in any training situation. People get very perplexed when the dog seems disinterested in the silver medal motivator when in other contexts it works so well. They talk about the dog being "distracted." If the dog is vigorously pursuing something and you're waving some lesser motivator at him, *you're* the distraction at that moment. It's important to understand that the motivational hierarchy is in constant flux, depending on availability and internal states that are in turn influenced by satiation and deprivation levels. A trainer must always have control of the top motivator in order to train.

Here's an example. After playing for an hour at the dog park and sniffing the ground for twenty minutes on the way there, a dog who has not eaten since the night before may find food to be the gold medal motivator. His clone, who lives next door, just had an enormous breakfast and hasn't played with another dog for days, nor been for a walk, pottying only in the yard for the same time period. The gold medal for this dog is likely to be other dogs. If none are around, the silver medal, scents on the ground, is promoted to gold. The trainer can manipulate availability of motivators as well as deprivation/satiation levels and this is an extremely important part of behavior modification. No motivation, no training.

In the case of on-leash manners for Tarzan, the key variables to include in the operant criteria setting are: degree of dog-dog satiation (i.e. how long was the play-session preceding the manners session?), familiarity of other dog, warm-up (i.e. how long after the play session and/or previous trial is the current exercise) and possibly the other dog's demeanor, along with the usual parameters of distance, location, degree of prompting and who's handling.

If, because of bite inhibition or recruiting problems, he isn't getting any remedial socialization, use some hard aerobic exercise in place of play sessions. This produces some fatigue, which although inferior to the satiation effects combined with exercise obtained with dog-dog play, is better than nothing. If the other dog's demeanor matters (i.e. passive Vs. outgoing Vs. threatening), include it. Likewise location. Although it's not formally included in the exercises below, it's a good idea to vary this, except when stuck.

Don't gloss over the prompt-fad task at the very first level. If you find yourself resorting to prompts at later stages, it's a sign that either the behavior was not sufficiently fluent (and prompt-free) in initial training, or else you're trying to progress too fast. Polish up the basic loose-leash walking and/or sits, or back off on other parameters rather than regressing to lures in later training.

Once the dog makes contact for each exercise, allow a brief mutual investigation and then break them off with happy talk and, if he's interested, a treat. Repeat until he's extremely ho-hum about the dog. A good sign to move on to a harder level is that he starts playing you for the food rewards and has to be encouraged to investigate the other dog. Plan sessions ahead of time and keep records so that, if you make fast progress, you can have appropriate dogs ready in any given session. The following is a relatively comprehensive set of criteria rungs. Some levels will require many repetitions and multiple sessions and others you will skip altogether. Every case is different. If he's sailing along, skip levels at your discretion. If in doubt, go slow, doing all levels. I like parallel walks very much. They can provide an additional bridge between those sessions that take place immediately after play and those with some cool off, or other sticky parts in the hierarchy. Walk the target and stimulus dog together on leash for ten or fifteen minutes and then practice meet and greets (this will obviously necessitate them coming together for the walk, which will be less attractive than the post-walk exercises).

Parameter 1: Satiation

Level 1

Satiation:	25-30 minute play session
Familiarity:	Maximum – dog from play session used
Warm-up:	Maximum – manners session commences immediately after play session
Prompting:	Maximum at start of session - visible food lure, visual access to other dog blocked by body if necessary – fade to final desired level by end of session

Level 2

Satiation:	15-20 minute play session
Familiarity:	Maximum – dog from play session used
Warm-up:	Maximum – manners session commences immediately after play session
Prompting:	Low

Level 3

Satiation: 10 minute play session
Familiarity: Maximum – dog from play session used
Warm-up: Maximum – manners session commences
               immediately after play session
Prompting: Low

Level 4

Satiation: 5 minute play session
Familiarity: Maximum – dog from play session used
Warm-up: Maximum – manners session commences
               immediately after play session
Prompting: Low

Level 5

Satiation   1 – 2 minute play session
Familiarity: Maximum – dog from play session used
Warm-up: Maximum – manners session commences
               immediately after play session
Prompting: Low

Switch to…

Parameter 2: Familiarity

Level 1

Satiation: Maximum – 20-30 minute play session
Familiarity: Moderate – familiar dog but one not in play
               session that just finished
Warm-up: Maximum – manners session commences
               immediately after play session
Prompting: Low

Level 2

Satiation: Maximum – 20-30 minute play session
Familiarity: Difficult – novel dog (include dog variables
               here if incorporating these)
Warm-up: Maximum – manners session commences
               immediately after play session
Prompting: Low

Switch to…

Parameter 1 & 2 Combo: Satiation & Familiarity

Level 1

Satiation: Moderate - 10-minute play session
Familiarity: Moderate – familiar dog but one not in play
               session that just finished
Warm-up: Maximum – manners session commences
               immediately after play session
Prompting: Low

Level 2

Satiation: Low - 5-minute play session
Familiarity: Moderate – familiar dog but one not in play
               session that just finished
Warm-up: Maximum – manners session commences
               immediately after play session
Prompting: Low

Level 3

Satiation: Very low – 1-2-minute play session
Familiarity: Moderate – familiar dog but one not in play
               session that just finished
Warm-up: Maximum – manners session commences
               immediately after play session
Prompting: Low

Level 4

Satiation:	Moderate - 10-minute play session
Familiarity:	Moderate – familiar dog but one not in play session that just finished
Warm-up:	Maximum – manners session commences immediately after play session
Prompting:	Low

Level 5

Satiation:	Moderate - 10-minute play session
Familiarity:	Difficult – novel dog
Warm-up:	Maximum – manners session commences immediately after play session
Prompting:	Low

Level 6

Satiation:	Low - 5-minute play session
Familiarity:	Difficult – novel dog
Warm-up:	Maximum – manners session commences immediately after play session
Prompting:	Low

Level 7

Satiation:	Very low – 1-2-minute play session
Familiarity:	Difficult – novel dog
Warm-up:	Maximum – manners session commences immediately after play session
Prompting:	Low

Switch to…

Parameter 3: Warm-up

Level 1

Satiation: Maximum - 25-30 minute play session
Familiarity: Maximum – dog from play session used
Warm-up: Moderate – manners session commences 15-30 minutes after end of play session and dogs separated
Prompting: Low

Level 2

Satiation: Maximum - 25-30 minute play session
Familiarity: Maximum – dog from play session used
Warm-up: Cooled off – manners session commences 1-2 hours after end of play session and dogs separated
Prompting: Low

Level 3

Satiation: Maximum - 25-30 minute play session
Familiarity: Maximum – dog from play session used
Warm-up: Semi-cold – manners session commences 4+ hours after end of play session and dogs separated
Prompting: Low

Level 4

Satiation: 25-30 minute play session previous day
Familiarity: Maximum – dog from session previous day
Warm-up: Cold – no play session that day
Prompting: Low

Switch to…

Satiation, Familiarity and Warm-Up Combo

Level 1

Satiation: Moderate: 10-minute play session
Familiarity: Maximum – dog from play session used
Warm-up: Moderate – manners session commences
              15-30 minutes after end of play session and
              dogs separated
Prompting: Low

Level 2

Satiation: Low: 5-minute play session
Familiarity: Maximum – dog from play session used
Warm-up: Moderate – manners session commences
              15-30 minutes after end of play session and
              dogs separated
Prompting: Low

Level 3

Satiation: Very low: 1-2-minute play session
Familiarity: Maximum – dog from play session used
Warm-up: Moderate – manners session commences
              15-30 minutes after end of play session and
              dogs separated
Prompting: Low

Level 4

Satiation: Moderate: 10-minute play session
Familiarity: Moderate: familiar dog but one not in earlier
              play session
Warm-up: Moderate – manners session commences
              15-30 minutes after end of play session and
              dogs separated
Prompting: Low

Level 5

Satiation:	Moderate: 10-minute play session
Familiarity:	Difficult – novel dog
Warm-up:	Moderate – manners session commences 15-30 minutes after end of play session and dogs separated
Prompting:	Low

Level 6

Satiation:	Low: 5-minute play session
Familiarity:	Difficult – novel dog
Warm-up:	Moderate – manners session commences 15-30 minutes after end of play session and dogs separated
Prompting:	Low

Level 7

Satiation:	Very low: 1-2-minute play session
Familiarity:	Difficult – novel dog
Warm-up:	Moderate – manners session commences 15-30 minutes after end of play session and dogs separated
Prompting:	Low

Level 8

Satiation:	Moderate: 10-minute play session
Familiarity:	Moderate: familiar dog but one not in earlier play session
Warm-up:	Cooled off - manners session commences 1-2 hours after end of play session and dogs separated
Prompting:	Low

Level 9

Satiation: Moderate: 10-minute play session
Familiarity: Moderate: familiar dog but one not in earlier play session
Warm-up: Semi-cold – manners session commences 4+ hours after end of play session and dogs separated
Prompting: Low

Level 10

Satiation: Moderate: 10-minute play session previous day
Familiarity: Moderate: familiar dog but one not in previous day's play session
Warm-up: Cold – no play session that day
Prompting: Low

Level 11

Satiation: Moderate: 10-minute play session previous day
Familiarity: Moderate: familiar dog but one not in previous day's play session
Warm-up: Cold – no play session that day
Prompting: Low

Level 12

Satiation: Moderate: 10-minute play session previous day
Familiarity: Difficult – novel dog
Warm-up: Cold – no play session that day
Prompting: Low

At this stage, the dog is meeting a novel dog cold, having had a brief play session the previous day, and so is ready for most encounters in day to day life.

Growly Dog Classes

A competently run obedience course usually addresses walking on leash and some may even practice meeting other dogs. A good growly dog class will almost certainly address this. This may prove the best option if the growly class is well run and if recruiting prospects unpromising. The signs of a good growly dog class are:

❑ High ratio of instructors to students – these classes need thorough one on one coaching to avoid mishap and to install the basic skills in the handlers

❑ Careful screening of participants – screening out any dog-human aggression, known hard mouths and types of dog aggression that would not benefit from the exercises taught in class

❑ Impeccable environmental management – use of barriers, distance, carefully orchestrated entries and exits from the class keep the dogs successful

❑ Techniques are derived from operant and classical concepts and put in easy to understand language

❑ Non-aversive techniques

Resolving Proximity Sensitivity

Dogs that have had limited experience with other dogs and present as fearful – avoidance, flight - are usually easy for owners to identify with. What owners sometimes need help understanding are fearful dogs who present as asocial and snappy or, worse, pre-emptive lungers. The latter can look very "confident," and explaining to the owner that the underlying motivation is fear is a crucial first step.

This is because improving their behavior requires getting at the underlying uncomfortable emotional state. Some of these dogs have had histories of feckless attempts at reprimanding by their owners, which often exacerbates the problem. Enter Pavlov.

Principles of Desensitization and Counterconditioning

Systematic desensitization and *counterconditioning* (D&C) are usually used together to treat fear and anxiety related problems. Desensitization refers to a careful manipulation of the intensity of the fear-evoking thing, in this case the other dog, so that it doesn't generate a fear response. It's helpful to think of it as a breaking of the association between the scary dog and the emotional response. No matter what one is afraid of, there's likely a version of it – smaller, very far away, very carefully controlled – that won't trigger the fear.

Right after this much less intense version of the scary dog is presented, a pleasant thing – the counterconditioning stimulus – is presented, to build a new association. This may be tasty food or a favorite game. It must be extremely potent. Many years ago, Bill Campbell wrote of the "jolly routine," wherein aggressive dogs were giggled at and jollied, rather than punished. The happy, silly voice does seem to make a significant difference, even for dogs who are not necessarily praise junkies. It may be because it gives the owner an alternative to tense admonitions and reprimands, has come to predict all manner of good things, or simply sets a relaxed tone. Nobody knows, but because it works so well, modeling and coaching owners at its execution is vital.

The process of presenting the scary stimulus dog at reduced threshold followed immediately by jolly talk and food or game is repeated until, whenever the scary dog (at reduced intensity) appears, the dog being treated feels a positive anticipation of the food or game before it has been actually initiated. This informs the trainer that a CER – Conditioned Emotional Response – now exists. Once the CER is evident, the intensity of the scary thing is very, very gradually raised and the process repeated until the CER is again evident. Eventually the full throttle version of the original scary dog is reached but now the dog feels no fear. In its place is the new happy association with the pleasant thing it has come to predict.

When stimuli are presented in this reduced intensity form for desensitization purposes, it is called a "sub-threshold" presentation. The threshold being referred to is the point at which the dog starts to feel the fear. If, at any point, the dog shows the original reaction to the trigger, it means the intensity of the presentation is "*super*-threshold." It is important to then back off to a reduced trigger intensity and work back up gradually again. Not only can going over threshold slow progress down, it can often cause regressions. If the dog feels any of the real fear, the trainer is no longer performing desensitization. Desensitization is, by definition, working sub-threshold.

Recognizing the Presence of a CER

At the Academy, one of the assignments in the animal learning course is to establish a CER to a neutral object in one of the shelter dogs. Students audition the object to ascertain that it does not elicit any response and then proceed to condition it to some potent, novel food item or favorite game. The unconditioned response (UCR) that the dog has to the food treat or game usually includes elements such as tail wagging, pupil dilation and salivation. The response to the previously neutral object (CS) post-conditioning often has the same elements but may also include orientation to where the dog thinks the UCR is going to come from. This is because the value of the CS is its ability to predict, "it's time for IT!!!" where IT is the potent food or game.

So, when trying to gauge whether a dog has a CER, look for things such as wagging, salivating (if you are using food as a counterconditioning stimulus) and alert, happy anticipation. When owners say, "wanna cookie??" to their dog or "walkies!" the response in dogs that "know" the word is a classic example of a CER. The words were previously neutral but came to predict a potent thing – cookies or walks.

Well-executed desensitization and counterconditioning is a magical thing to witness. A dog that dislikes the presence and proximity of other dogs now feels happy and relaxed when they are around. Once the discomfort is alleviated, the snarling, snapping and lunging resolve. It's easy to see that, although it may be possible to suppress the same behaviors with strong enough punishment, the underlying fear and dislike of other dogs remains, only now the dog is in a bind. Feel that awful feeling or face the aversive.

The counterconditioning aspect represents an application of Pavlovian (or Classical) conditioning. Unlike the more familiar operant conditioning, where dogs learn about the relationship between their own behavior and its consequences, Pavlovian conditioning teaches dogs about the relationship between events occurring out there in the world. If there is a predictive order – as there often is in the real world – many, many animals will learn this. There are distinct advantages to learning about tip-offs: "Whenever this happens, that happens next…"

While many owners and trainers grasp that increasing distance between a frightened dog and whatever is scaring her is good practice, what turns this informal measure into bona fide conditioning is the careful manipulation of distance as well as other variables to *maintain* a sub-threshold intensity, a systematic finely graded hierarchy that is strictly adhered to, the addition of consistent and properly timed counterconditioning, and regular practice sessions with multiple pairings. When one of these elements is not properly executed, the technique fails.

D&C Hierarchy Construction

Along with the usual hierarchy elements of distance and duration, there are a few variables that are enormously helpful to manipulate stimulus intensity:

- ❑ How passive the stimulus dog is – still Vs. moving

- ❑ Size of stimulus dog

- ❑ Freedom of asocial dog to manipulate distance and speed of approach to stimulus dog

- ❑ Orientation of stimulus dog (rear pointed at asocial)

- ❑ Number of stimulus dogs

Hmm…this end is not as scary

Let's see how these puzzle pieces fit together in a real hierarchy.

Sample D&C Hierarchy for Proximity Sensitivity

In the following, note that if one parameter is made more difficult, the others are kept the same or relaxed. This may remind you of the criteria juggling during behavior shaping, D&C's operant cousin. Only proceed to the next step when the dog being worked on demonstrates a clear "where's my snack/game!" anticipatory reaction when the stimulus dog is presented. Failing to do so is known as "skating on thin ice" and will eventually catch up to you. It's not enough that the dog is not responding noticeably fearfully – go for the evident positive CER. Long duration sessions are the most productive. Don't forget the jolly talk and super high-value treats.

1) Passive, still, restrained dog at twenty feet

2) Same dog at 15 feet

3) Same dog at 10 feet

4) Same dog moving at 15 feet

5) Same dog moving at 10 feet

6) Same dog still at 6 feet with investigation option: restrained and oriented away from proximity sensitive dog for long period. Proximity sensitive dog clicked and treated for any investigation or approach. This includes sniffing, stretch investigations, wake-sniffing or even looking at the other dog. It's very important at that you've been using a passive dog so that, at this step, he does not "punish" the proximity sensitive dog with overtures of his own

7) Same dog does 24-48 hour sleep-over/dog-sitting at proximity sensitive dog's house

8) Same dog on leash meet and greets with jolly talk and clicks and treats for any investigation

9) Repeat steps 1 – 8 with a new passive dog

10) Repeat steps 1 – 8 with another new passive dog

11) "Play group" between the three dogs – an off-leash session on neutral turf. There may not be any play whatsoever, only mutual boredom. Do not be deterred. The goal with these dogs is increased comfort, not dog-craziness. Play is a rare bonus. Continue to click and treat any interest in the dogs

12) Repeat steps 1-6 with novel dogs that are more outgoing (note: outgoing, not Tarzan)

After completing the hierarchy to the six-foot distance, commence cold trial on-leash passes with brand new dogs, taking care to not get closer than six feet. In the unlikely event that play has broken out with any of the dogs used in hierarchy work, continue regular play sessions with that dog(s) if possible. You may also elect to do steps 7 and 8 with the more outgoing dogs, especially if play did break out. If the sleep-overs and close meet and greets seem over-threshold, back off to safer, passive dogs for a longer period and protect the proximity sensitive dog from spontaneous encounters with the outgoing sorts.

Very severe cases may benefit from a course of anti-anxiety medication in conjunction with the D&C to maximize gains. Once the dog has gone up the hierarchy to the point of successful cold trials and possibly meet and greets with less passive dogs, the medication should be gradually tapered off. Keep in mind that the use of psychotropics for these types of problems is a field in its infancy. It often requires some trial and error to find an agent that confers clear benefit.

Counterconditioning Without Desensitization

It is always preferable to use counterconditioning in conjunction with carefully graded exposure, however, if this cannot be achieved all of the time, sometimes mileage can be gained by counterconditioning even when the dog goes off. One example would be when there is no pool or extremely limited pool of dogs to work with. Another example is occasional (or regular!) management lapses. This technique can appear astounding to the casual observer as it looks like the trainer is rewarding the dog for lunging, snarling, snapping etc.

In spite of it being "operant-counterintuitive," when super-threshold exposure does happen, the owner should be instructed to jolly the dog and present the pleasant counter-stimulus as usual, regardless of the dog's reaction. The reason for this is the ultra-high priority of preserving what's called predictability in classical conditioning.

Predictability

Consider the two classical conditioning sessions on page 70. Trainer one has completed twice as many trials, however, the best tip-off that the counter-stimulus is on the way may not be the presence of a dog. The bait pouch, smell of bait and trainer's presence are equally predictive, as is the temporal regularity – trials are happening in a steady rhythm. It is likely that, if the dog has any prior experience being trained, the already learned tip-offs will block the new tip-off, even though in the trainer's mind, this is the important one.

Trainer two, by contrast, has fewer trials but has invested some time in ruling out these competing stimuli with "dead time" – time in which the smell of the bait, the trainer and the pouch are all present but no treats are furnished. This better isolates the dog's appearance as sold predictor of food. Trainer two has also arranged a trial after the official session is over and the dog is being walked home by the owner. The owner is given a small flip-top tin of delicious cat food – which has no smell preview – and a dog is presented out of "training session" context (at sub-threshold intensity, as always). The cat food is furnished immediately after the dog is perceived. In this trial, there is no trainer, bait pouch or smell of bait, but the dog = tasty food association is maintained. It is ultimately more efficient to pay careful attention to how good a predictor dogs are compared to competing predictors, than to simply crank out trials in a rhythmic fashion.

Yippee...I love it when she wears that pouch and faces me like that

Don't you love it when dogs are close by?

Predictability in Classical Conditioning

Trainer One				
Pairings and lulls	Trainer present	Bait pouch	Smell of bait	Dog present
Trial 1	X	X	X	X
Trial 2	X	X	X	X
Trial 3	X	X	X	X
Trial 4	X	X	X	X
Trial 5	X	X	X	X
Trial 6	X	X	X	X
Etc.	X	X	X	X

Trainer Two				
Pairings and lulls	Trainer present	Bait pouch	Smell of bait	Dog present
No food furnished for 20 minutes	X	X	X	
Trial 1	X	X	X	X
15 min break – no food	X	X	X	
Trial 2	X	X	X	X
5 min break	X	X	X	
Trial 3 - Post session surprise: dog=canned cat food	·			X

Operant Mindset Vs. Classical Conditioning

This predictability is most definitely marred in training if the trainer slips into operant mode and only "rewards" the dog contingent on desired behavior. What ends up happening is that, in a percentage of trials (and, notably, in those trials where the dog was clearly in the problem category – the original reaction was elicited), the counter-stimulus is not forthcoming. This muddies the classical waters. There are no "schedules" in classical conditioning, only weak or partial conditioning, which is inferior.

The bottom line is if you're attempting classical conditioning, your highest priority is preserving the association between two stimuli. Disregard the dog's behavior. In those cases where stimulus intensity can't be controlled, this means furnishing to a dog who is demonstrating problem behavior.

Operant Exercises for Proximity Sensitive Dogs

An alternative technique for dogs that are uncomfortable around other dogs is to teach them to do something around other dogs that is incompatible with retreating or behaving aggressively. There are advantages to using operant rather than classical conditioning. They are:

1) It is more intuitive for most owners and trainers to focus on getting a behavior than on arranging stimuli

2) The dog's willingness to perform for food or toys provides an easier gauge of the dog's comfort level – if the other dog(s) is too close, performance and interest in reinforcement will deteriorate

3) If the dog already has had training with positive reinforcement, there is likely a built-in CER to the

training set-up. This jump starts a free CER to the other dog's presence, provided the session is initiated after the other dog appears (to ensure that other dogs predict the fun session, rather than vice-versa, which would not help the cause)

 For example, a dog can be taught to sit and make eye contact with the handler. The behavior should first be taught and perfected out of context, i.e with no other dogs around. The behavior should then be proofed for routine distractions – new locations, cold (out of the blue with surprise hidden reinforcers) trials during walks, in places with human pedestrian traffic. When it is reliable in these situations, dogs can be introduced. The distance and other intensity factors should be monitored as during classical conditioning, only now the dog is being reinforced for correct responses of the sit and watch, rather than contingent on the other dog's presence.

Sit and watch is easy to teach but is not the only behavior that would work. Spinning in a circle, lying down, waving, sitting up or any fun trick would be suitable. Depending on the individual dog, a trick incorporating more movement might keep the dog loose, play into an urge to actively do something and/or simply be enjoyable. Lying down serves as an extra gauge of comfort level as anxious dogs are less likely to do it. Beware however of immobilizing the hyper-obedient type.

If the criteria is properly set to achieve a very high rate of reinforcement, the presence of the other dog(s) comes to predict the game and attendant reinforcement. This functions as bonus classical counterconditioning. The potential classical collateral effects of operant conditioning will be a "yippee!" type CER if the trainer is employing positive reinforcement and a fear CER if the trainer employs aversives.

This is one of the primary arguments in favor of the use of positive reinforcement, as opposed to the use of aversives such as collar corrections, squirt bottles etc. Although it is possible to teach dogs that it is dangerous for them to behave aggressively, the underlying discomfort around other dogs, if this was the original motivation, is not addressed and likely worsened by the aversive technique. Ian Dunbar calls this "removing the ticker from the time bomb."

Raising criteria would consist of making the other dog's distance gradually smaller or the intensity gradually greater. Variables similar to those that serve in counterconditioning hierarchies can help out here too. Whereas in classical counterconditioning, these were hierarchy variables, now they are criteria variables:

❑ Other dog social passivity and movement

❑ Size of other dog

❑ Orientation of other dog (rear pointed at asocial)

❑ Number of other dogs

Sample OC Rungs for Proximity Sensitivity

Dogs that are proximity sensitive can also be taught to target other dogs. This is fiendishly clever as it has all the advantages of operant conditioning I listed above and guarantees perception of the other dog occurring prior to reinforcer delivery, thus enhancing the classical side effect.

The first step is to clicker condition the dog. Good timing is vital for this exercise. It may be worth practicing a couple of free-shaping sessions before tackling the dog-targeting problem. This way the dog has a bit of experience with being shaped. The following is a list of possible criteria rungs (C/T = click and treat). *Be sure to use a passive stimulus dog for the early levels.*

Level One: Passive dog restrained

1. C/T for head-turn in direction of other dog

2. C/T orientation toward other dog

3. C/T any movement – leaning or steps – toward other dog

4. C/T for closer and closer proximity

5. C/T nose-targeting somewhere on other dog's body (dog's choice where)

6. Two or three nose-targets per C/T

7. Duration: must hang out 4 or 5 seconds next to other dog (nose prods optional)

8. Duration: must hang out 6 – 10 seconds next to other dog (nose prods optional)

Level Two: Moving target. Repeat steps 1 – 8 with the same passive dog but now while he is moved around on leash

Level Three: New dog. Repeat steps 1 – 8 with a novel passive dog (restrained if necessary)

Level Four: Moving target. Repeat steps 1 – 8 with dog from level three, now allowed to move freely

Level Five: Two moving targets. Repeat steps 1 – 8 with both dogs used above moving freely

Level Six: More outgoing dog, restrained. Repeat steps 1 – 8 with a new, more active dog but kept in one area on leash

Level Seven: Moving outgoing target. Repeat steps 1 – 8 with dog from level six, now allowed to move freely

Level Eight: Get behavior on cue and proceed to practice around safe dogs

Getting behavior on cue means the dog's performance is reliable when cued and does not happen when the cue is not given. The main reason for being sticky about stimulus control is to avoid the dog, who now knows and loves the dog-targeting game, trundling up to an unfriendly or overly boisterous dog, which could be aversive. You'll need some control over when the behavior is offered.

Protect gains by scrupulously avoiding bad experiences with other dogs. This means screening the company s/he keeps with some care. Most proximity sensitive dogs can be made more comfortable and therefore less aggressive around other dogs, and a few become affiliative, even playing. The outcome depends on diligence, exercise execution, avoidance of bad experiences and initial severity.

Combining Classical and Operant Conditioning

Aside from the collateral classical counterconditioning in operant conditioning with a high rate of reinforcement, the techniques can be deliberately mixed and matched in a given case. For instance, a case I recently worked on began with some orchestrated D&C sessions, along with solo counterconditioning on regular walks between sessions as the dog went off easily and managing the presence of other dogs proved too difficult in an urban environment. When the lunge rate went down, we switched to an operant exercise – sit or down with watch.

This is a great first-line-of-defense formula for extremely explosive dogs.

Medication

In those cases where a dog's fear is severe, an anti-anxiety medication may help facilitate the behavior modification process, regardless of whether a classical or operant approach is being employed. The drug can be commenced prior to the start of exercises to achieve an adequate blood level. This can sometimes take several weeks, so must be planned for. Drugs in the anti-depressant/anti-obsessional class, including selective serotonin re-uptake inhibitors such as Prozac, Paxil, Luvox, Zoloft, and tri-cyclics such as Clomicalm and Elavil, seem to hold the most promise. At present, it is not possible to know in advance which particular agent will work on an individual dog's neurochemistry, so a trial and error process may be necessary. Unfortunately, veterinary use of most of these medication is currently off-label, which can hamper willingness on the part of general practice veterinarians to prescribe.

Affiliative Behaviors and Meta-Communication

When observing dog interactions, a good predictor of low likelihood of aggression is the presence of signs of affiliation or relaxed friendliness. The absence of these behaviors is glaring and usually a sign of problems to ensue.

So, aside from an absence of growling, snarling and fighting, the following is a list of what we are looking for when two dogs meet:

- ❑ Relaxed facial expression on approach

- ❑ Investigation of head and rear areas

- ❑ Allowing investigation of head and rear areas

- ❑ Continual movement during investigation, i.e. little "waxiness"

- ❑ Simultaneous mutual rear investigation - circle investigation

- ❑ Rapid segue of investigation into play or voluntary withdrawal, to go separate ways or to urinate

- ❑ Elbow bends – pawing and paw raises

- ❑ Lip licking or tongue flicking

- ❑ Freezing in one dog if the other dog stands over – this is most familiar in the T-position configuration but also can occur at more subtle angles as well as muzzle to muzzle

Note that speed and intensity of approach are not mentioned. Fast, excited approaches can be friendly and they can be aggressive. Hackles (erection of the hair on the neck, withers, back and/or rump) are a sign of sympathetic nervous system activation and thus not great news but ambiguous - their absence is too weak an indicator to hang your hat on.

There are other parameters, such as tail position, making oneself "small" or "big," body orientation and eye contact, that sometimes precede trouble and other times lead to peaceful meetings or play. "Flag tail," for instance, is held vertically and is often seen in conjunction with a high frequency, low amplitude wag. Associated with courtship, it is also regularly seen during meet & greets. The dog may be standing for investigation or performing a mutual investigation. Flag tails with no wag tend to be more ambiguous – sometimes in the context just described and sometimes in a dog on the verge of fighting.

This is a great example of how cautious one must be when trying to decipher dog body language. The inference of internal states is very fertile ground for subjective interpretation. You can never know what is going on inside another organism's head. This doesn't stop (or even slow down) the veritable cottage industry in "reading dogs." Be especially wary of non-falsifiable mind reading or of exclusive emphasis on one body part such as the belief that the exact location of hackles has particular meaning.

Before discussing resolution of bullying and play-skill deficits, both of which manifest in a dog with play history, it's necessary to know what normal dog play looks like.

Play

During play and immediately preceding it, look for the presence of play meta-signals (Dunbar's "atmosphere cues), which qualify the play behavior following it. There is a continual stream of these punctuating playful interactions. The reason so much play behavior needs qualifying has to do with the significant overlap with agonistic behavior and hunting. If you think about it, play consists of biting, chasing, wrestling and body slamming. Meta-signals say, "I'm about to bite (chase, slam, pin…) you but it's just for play." Very important function. The atmosphere cues seen in dog play are:

- Bouncy, inefficient movements, gamboling

- Sudden, explosive feints, as though enticing chase

- Play face – panting, "grinning" mouth, ears up high and often rotated backwards, eye whites frequently visible

- Play bows - front end down, rear up, often done in "shorthand" where there is only the faintest suggestion of this posture

Bullying and Play Skill Deficits

When dogs are playing and the play becomes unpleasant for one of the participants, the non-consenting dog will either perform some appeasement behavior – rolling over, tail-tucking and/or licking for instance – or else stop and demonstrate some threat gesture such as snarling or snapping. Sometimes the stressed dog may just try to evade his tormentor. Most playmates receiving this kind of communication will briefly cease playing, play more tentatively or otherwise shift gear. Occasionally, especially  when delivered to a less experienced dog, it will take an escalated appeasement gesture or threat to get the message across. But the message gets across and play attempts cease or gears are shifted.

Bullies and dogs with play skill deficits both engage in some normal play. Bullies, however, target certain dogs for harassment or attack. They rarely play normally with these dogs yet play fine with others. When harassing a target, bullies tend to bulldoze past the target's shorthand appeasement gestures and threats and sometimes ignore even the scaled up versions. Fights often ensue.

Dogs with play skill deficits, by contrast, do not single out any particular dog. They start playing normally, though often intensely. Their play is characterized by a relative absence of demeanor shifting and atmosphere cues. They get more and more amped up, self-handicap very little and seem to get stuck in a rut, such as "bite bite bite bite," "chase chase chase chase" or "bodyslam bodyslam bodyslam bodyslam…" The dog on the receiving end tries turning the broken record off with appeasement and/or threat to no avail and a fight ensues. When this happens, it is known as an interaction "tipping over" from play into a fight.

The critical difference between a bully and a dog with a play skill deficit is the targeting of a specific dog for immediate attack or harassment Vs. play commencing normally and then tipping over as it heats up. The reason it is necessary to draw this distinction is that the resolution intervention differs depending on which a dog presents with. In both cases, the operant technique negative punishment will be employed, but the play skill deficit dog will have some sessions of prompted interruption before negative punishment (P-) is brought into the picture.

Use of Negative Punishment

Negative punishment is the reduction in frequency or intensity of behavior due to the termination of a reinforcing event. Human examples include penalty boxes in hockey, penalties in lost yardage in football, fines (removal of money, a perfectly generalized conditioned reinforcer) and disallowing a teenager from socializing outside for a given period of time.

It is important to contrast this with positive punishment, which is the reduction in frequency or intensity of behavior due to the introduction of an aversive. Smacking, leash jerking, pinning and electric shock are all examples of stimuli that have been used in dog training to positively punish dogs. The potency of aversives lies in their evoking fear of bodily injury or death. The collateral effects of aversives – fear and its associated body states, classically conditioned associations to elements in the stimulus package at the time of the aversive and, in some cases, exacerbated aggression – render it very, very harmful.

People are frequently confused by the question of distress to the dog and the similarity in name (and effect on behavior) of the two sorts of punishment. Both, by definition, decrease behavior. Both work best on a continuous schedule (i.e. every instance of the target behavior is punished). The less favorable side-effect profile, however, belongs to positive punishment, due to the presence of an aversive stimulus. Both aversives and termination of reinforcers are motivating, but there is a vital difference between being really, really peeved or disappointed and fearing for one's bodily integrity. The increasing number and sophistication of non-aversive training techniques will sooner or later relegate positive punishment to the history books.

In dog training, negative punishment is extremely potent in those cases where the trainer has good control of the dog's access to his top motivator at that moment. In other words, you really have the dog. Classic examples are timing puppies out for hard play-biting by exiting the confinement area, abruptly terminating tug games when the dog is sloppy with his jaws or breaks a rule and snatching a dangled treat or toy away when a dog breaks a stay (and then supplying the same goodie when the dog refrains from breaking).

Negative Punishment for Bullying

Dogs that bully other dogs find both play and harassment/fighting to be reinforcing events, so timing them out for harassment and fighting is extremely effective at reducing these. The tricky part is the orchestration in vast spaces, such as at dog parks. Before getting into dealing with this messy business, let's go over the basic time-out mechanics.

Dogs are very good at flow charts. The negative punishment flow chart looks like this:

Note that there is one warning kicking off the two possible contingencies. By far the most frequent error in time-out execution is the provision of multiple warnings, often of gradually escalating intensity. ("That's enough...That's e-NOUGH!... I said that's ENOUGH... knock it off... NOW!... THAT'S ENOUGH!!!!!!!!!!!!!..."). In order for the warning to develop meaning, it must be followed by real consequences. In fact, if one wanted to systematically dilute one's warning cue, the way to do it would be to issue it without following it up with any primary consequences.

So, it is terribly important to cue and execute the time out when the dog ignores the warning. In early trials, he is guaranteed to ignore the warning, as it is still a meaningless cue. The time-out cue, typically something like "too bad" or "you're out," serves as a bridge to the primary punisher, the time-out, exactly the same way a conditioned reinforcer such as a clicker serves as a bridge to a primary reinforcer. Be sure to apply this conditioned negative punisher with good timing (the first naughty act after the warning cue is issued). I prefer to continue bridging until the dog is caught and in the penalty box or otherwise had his fun/freedom terminated.

The Messy Business

The faster the time-out can follow the bullying behavior and the conditioned negative punisher, the better. This can be logistically tricky, as bullying often occurs in free-play situations where the dog has plenty of maneuverability and may elect to stay out of reach, especially once he starts to learn the meaning of the conditioned punisher. However messy it is, it is imperative that the time-out happen, even if long after the transgression and initial bridge occurred. There are a few options to accomplish this.

The ideal way is to remove the other dogs in a timely fashion. This avoids any potential side effects from approaching and/or taking hold of the dog being trained. Although this side effect ends up being limited to occasions after the negative punishment marker is given, it is an important consideration.

Another solution is to simply track the bully down. Once "too bad" is issued, grimly follow the dog around until he is caught and I have employed grim track-downs on countless cases with excellent results. It seems quite counter-intuitive at first, as the dog appears to be having a good time dancing around out of reach, and the time-out feels ridiculously late (not to mention the last behavior being "letting himself be caught"). But, over trials, the dancing around diminishes (although note that it may get worse before it gets better), and the dog starts heeding the warning cue, which indicates that the contingencies are being learned. It is fatal to the cause to throw in the towel if you elect to do track-downs – always follow through.

I have often committed what might be considered an act of virtual heresy during this training. The very first time the dog refrains from dancing around after a time-out has been cued, I cancel the punishment. This is heresy because 1) punishment works best on a continuous schedule (and I have skipped one) and, worse, 2) the relationship between the conditioned negative punisher ("too bad") and the punishment is a classical one. There are no "schedules" in classical conditioning, only partial conditioning. This renders my issuing of the conditioned punisher followed by the failure to deliver the primary an extinction trial.

These facts notwithstanding, I suggest doing it once, perhaps twice, in cases where the dog was a chronic escape artist after being issued time-out cues. Don't fall into the trap of doing it more than once or twice as the dog will learn the new flow chart, which is: "I bully, ignore the warning, hear the time-out cue, turn myself in and get off the hook." The good news is that usually the dog turning himself in is the precursor to his heeding the warning cue in the first place. In other words, it's a tip-off to you that he's starting to learn the system. The time-out cue has power and so the warning acquires great meaning.

Another way to orchestrate time-outs is to arrange play sessions in early training in areas that do not allow as much dance-around option once the time-out cue has been given. A third is to have a couple of extra agents on hand to help. And, finally, long lines can be used in these sorts of procedures. There are two distinct disadvantages to the use of long lines. One is that they can become tangled in legs, catch on things, clothesline the dog, and tie dogs together in the thick of a fight, causing panic reactions. Because of this, I strongly advise not using one if you are not a good line wrangler. The other disadvantage is that the line is quite noticeable and so may mask the bullying. And, even if it doesn't, its high salience may mean a regression once the line comes off. In the case of bullying (as opposed to early work with play skill deficits), I'd use lines as a last resort only.

Negative punishment has popped up in popular dog training in various guises, including "No Change Responses" ®, "Abandonment Training" and so on. All involve the removal of some stimulus, be it an expected reaction from the owner or the owner him/herself. If the target behavior decreases as a result of the intervention, it is negative punishment, period.

Play Skill Deficits

Recall that the issue in play skill deficits is not target-specific. Dogs with play skill deficits do not exhibit normal play with any dogs. All their play is characterized by few to no atmosphere cues and few to no role reversals during play. They obviously enjoy playing and their more resilient playmates enjoy playing with them initially. During the course of play, the problem dog seems to become stuck on the same action, often with escalating intensity.

The other dog becomes non-consenting at some point, and the play turns into harassment or a fight.

Many such dogs play well as puppies and some play okay but roughly as puppies. Some tip over from puppyhood. The onset *tends* to be gradual and is full-blown by age 2 or 3. In sharp contrast to a Tarzan, which requires an impoverished socialization history, play skill deficits can occur in spite of heavy and carefully managed socialization to other dogs. Because of the over-representation of pit bulls and pit crosses in the ranks of dogs with play skill deficits, I would submit that there is a possible genetic component. Whether the mechanism is a watered down and/or partial version of the genetic suite that predispose pits to chronically fight, I know not, though I see how it tempting to think so.

Unlike bullies, who do well with operant contingencies immediately, dogs who play normally and then heat up do better with some sessions of coaching before the introduction of negative punishment.

Prompting Self-Interruption

Always use experienced, bulletproof dogs. The goal of these sessions is to teach the dog with the play skill deficit to slow him or herself down when play starts to heat up. Because this does not happen spontaneously, there are no opportunities for selective reinforcement. So, instead, you will interrupt and re-direct. Prompt the dog to break focus and change activity as soon as you see either of the following:

1) Absence of demeanor shifting ("stuck" activity) for more than 30 seconds

2) Disregarded signs of lack of consent from the other dog (e.g. tail down, snarling, ears pinned back, cowering, snapping, attempts to escape, appeasement gestures)

Start with a cue such as "slow down," "gentle please" or "give him a break" and then immediately follow this up with getting the stuck dog off his playmate and focused on you. If luring him out works, this is an option. If the dog won't be lured or there are over-riding considerations, such as any demonstrated potential for food or toy guarding, physically prompt him. You can physically prompt by gently taking his collar, or you reel him off his victim with a long line or leash. There is no denying that physical prompts are clunky and have the potential for aversive side effects, however it is imperative the dog come off the other dog before tipping over completely, and that the verbal cue predict an effective prompt.

Minimize the side effects by using only as much mechanical stuff as necessary to get the job done. Once the dog is off, for instance, try luring with food, toy and your best happy dog-trainer voice. Have as brief a duration of physical hauling as possible. But do get the job done. Cool him off for several seconds by doing a flurry of sits and downs or a watch-me game, and then calmly send him back to play. Monitor for the next need to interrupt.

The most hellacious players will need constant interruption. They can be taxing on the other dogs and on the trainer's patience so monitor these as well. If any of the other dogs show signs of being insufficiently bulletproof, get them away from the problem dog and onto a steady diet of more normal players.

There will come a time when you find yourself interrupting and re-directing less often. This is because the dog has begun to self-interrupt at the likely times. There is no magic. The mechanism is classical conditioning. The "feel" of heated up play has become a reliable predictor of the interruption and cool-off. The other thing you will notice around this time is that, even if the dog does not self-interrupt, you are less often having to physically prompt after giving the cue, as the cue now breaks the dog off on its own.

When the self-interruption is unmistakably occurring at least half the time compared to baseline, it's time to bring in the negative punishment flow-chart for the times the dog does not self-interrupt. So, when the dog self-interrupts, nothing happens and play continues. When play heats up or becomes non-consenting without self-interruption, issue the cue that used to precede the mechanical interruption. This cue is now a negative punishment warning cue. If the dog breaks off on his own after the cue, issue a "thank you" and continue monitoring for future transgression. If he remains stuck after the warning cue, instead of mechanically interrupting and cooling him off, administer a bona fide time-out, a removal for a minute or two, from the play area. Crating in a "penalty box," removing the dog from the room if indoors, putting the dog in the car or exiting the dog park and going home are all likely effective. The regime is now identical to that for a bullying dog.

Dog-Dog Resource Guarding

Resource guarding between dogs is ubiquitous. Most people with more than one dog have witnessed mundane threatening and scuffling over food, toys, bones and the owner's attention. It also occurs with regularity in dogs that are acquaintances and complete strangers. Most practitioners acknowledge that this is normal behavior. And most elect to not intervene when the fights are clean and relatively rare. I personally advise intervention when there are injurious fights or inflated frequency.

I am defining injurious fights as fights where there are puncture wounds inflicted, with the exception of shallow punctures to faces and muzzles. Even the cleanest of fighters might occasionally produce a facial laceration or bleeding ear. For the purposes of this book, "inflated frequency" means either that the dogs are battling a few times a day and/or the owner feels very strongly that there is a problem.

In this last case, be sure to distinguish an owner who really can't take the amount of posturing and scuffling from an owner who is distressed because they have no idea what normal is. For instance, some people consider all aggression abnormal and/or a reflection of something they did wrong. An owner with a couple of dogs with an otherwise decent relationship that posture or fight cleanly a couple of times per week over some coveted resource may call you in to do massive behavior modification, but I'd argue that the first order of business in such a case would be to educate the owner about normal dog behavior. If this assuages the owner's distress, some simple management around the hottest resources may be all that's needed.

So, when taking history, be sure to both objectively quantify what the dogs are doing as well as characterize the owner's take on what the dogs are doing. It is very much the practitioner's call how to balance the owner's perception after educating and normalizing, the effort and expense of intervention and the potential risks of non-intervention.

Resource Management

Management regimes are a vital part of behavior modification programs and are also a cheap and easy way to reduce frequency even if the decision has been made to not actively intervene. Standard management practice involves scrupulously avoiding the problem scenarios. For instance, if problems between the dogs in question involve interactions around high-value items such as marrow bones or meaty bones, dogs should be locked away from each other when these are provided. Be sure to confiscate all traces before re-introducing the dogs to each other's chewing areas. If mealtimes are tense, employ down-stays to keep dogs waiting at a less volatile distance from each other and feed dogs in different corners of the kitchen or, if necessary, at different places and times altogether. In most cases where the problem is limited to mealtime woes, I advise this sort of management only.

If the dogs are squabbling over toys, pick these all up for a while. When exercising or playing with toys with the dogs, do one dog at a time unless doing specific exercises. The goal is for all experiences around the disputed resources to be therapeutic ones. If the problem is harder to avoid, such as numerous sleeping locations and/or the owner, the path of least resistance may be to separate the dogs except during exercises.

A general animosity between the dogs sometimes develops secondary to frequent tension and battles over resources. It is especially important in these cases to max out all management options to avoid further poisoning the dogs' relationship with skirmishes. Tensions can become linked to the timing around certain resource-laden events. In these cases, it's worth unpacking them as this can usually be diminished or at least compartmentalized.

For example, I remember an interesting case I had years ago when I had two dogs in for training, both incidentally dog-dog food guarders. My own two border collies also guarded their food against other dogs, making four total for a period of a few weeks. While they were all cohabiting I managed them around mealtimes with crates, sit and down-stays, and fed them all in their own spots. The dogs got along famously at other times.

Each morning the routine was the same. We'd all go for a walk and then come back and get into our crates and stays while breakfast was being prepared. After a couple of days, there was some tension during this ritual. Grumbling, wrinkly faces across the room at each other and hard eyes.

Several days after that, I noticed some snarkiness as leashes were removed on the way into the house after the walk. Then, days later, dogs were posturing at each other commencing after the halfway point on the walk. The emotional response of Breakfast Around Other Dogs was bleeding backwards through time. The solution did not require any behavior mod whatsoever, simply changing that rigid routine leading up to breakfast. With a shared, Big Event breakfast time no longer led up to, the tension on and immediately after the morning walk evaporated.

As this example illustrates, it can be worth bearing in mind how tense resource situations may infect other events in a multi-dog household. If there are any reliable tip-offs that a valued resource is imminent, the emotional tension accompanying it can become conditioned to the tip-off. This can result in testiness seemingly without cause.

Guarding Modification – Technique Options

There are a few different strategies for improving resource guarding and any resulting general animosity between dogs. Your choice will depend on the specific players in the case and the owner's objectives. Let's look at the strategy choices and how you can mix and match them to specific case types.

1) Desensitization and Counterconditioning of Guarding Dog(s) – the guarder is gradually classically conditioned to love having the other dog around him in the formerly charged scenario
2) Operant Conditioning of Guarding Dog(s) – the guarder is taught an alternative response, such as to withdraw rather than threaten/fight in order to retain possession of a resource, and (optional) once that is in place, guarding is negatively punished by resource loss

3) Operant Conditioning of Non-Guarding Dog(s) – the dog being most frequently guarded against is taught to avoid the guarding dog when the latter has a resource

Desensitization and Counterconditioning

 The objective of the exercises is to teach the problem dog that the presence and proximity of the other dog(s) predicts good things, even (and especially!) around resources. As with all D&C, keeping the intensity of the stimulus below the threshold where the guarder begins to get tense accelerates progress. This means paying close attention to the proximity of other dog to the guarder. At no point should the guarder guard. If he does, it's a trainer error. Between sessions, manage ruthlessly. It is imperative the guarder is not triggered in day-to-day life. This may mean removing all resources or even sequestering the dogs from each other.

To do these exercises, both dogs need some semblance of a sit and down-stay. If these are not present, install them. Tethering can also be used to keep the dogs in position or for added security. When the dogs are more advanced, the tether can be dispensed with.

Exercise 1: Prepare a bowl of small, healthy, tasty treats. With no resources in the vicinity, sit both dogs a few feet away from each other. Give a treat to the non-guarding dog first, followed immediately by lavish praise and a treat for the guarder. Pause several seconds. Repeat, always giving to the non-guarder first. If at any point, the guarder snarls, tries to muscle in on the other dog's treat or breaks the stay, sit the dogs a little further apart. Get under threshold.

If the owner is the contentious resource, employ whatever distance between the dogs is necessary to avoid tension. This may mean tethering one or both dogs to avoid sudden proximity should one break their stay. The likelihood is that the dogs will be so far apart that the owner must travel between dogs to deliver treats. This is fine. Commence the lavish praise to the guarder once the treat is delivered to the other dog and continue bridging until the treat is finally delivered to the guarder.

To achieve the best predictability, recall that long and varied inter-trial latencies are most effective. Avoid yo-yoing in a steady rhythm between one dog and the other with the treats. Continue the exercise until you see a clear anticipatory response (CER) from the guarder as soon as you feed the other dog. This may be very quick to come as many dogs in multi-dog households have already learned that when one dog gets something, chances are excellent they will too. It can also take a few sessions, which is fine.

If the dogs have been worked apart for this exercise, once the CER is in place, gradually move them closer together until they are a couple of feet apart. At any sign of tension from the guarder, increase distance and do more repetitions, then inch them closer again.

Exercise 2: Sit in a closed room with the guarder and a supply of tasty treats. The other dog is locked out and there are no hot resources in the room. Spend a good, long time (20-30 minutes) doing nothing with the dog. The ideal thing is to work on the computer, read or keep otherwise occupied. After this introductory period, open the door and bring the other dog into the room. As soon as the other dog is in the room, sit him or her, reinforce with a treat and then lavish praise and several treats on the guarder. Continue for twenty or thirty seconds, then remove the other dog from the room, put away the treats and go back to work, ignoring the guarder.

Let some time elapse and then repeat the procedure. Carry on until you once again see a clear anticipatory "yippee" style response from the guarder when the other dog appears. This may take anywhere from a few trials to a few sessions. When the CER is evident, repeat the exercise in as many different rooms as you can, always opening up the treat bar to the guarder when the other dog enters the room and closing it when he exits. Pay attention to the order of events, always bringing the other dog into the room before reaching for bait or otherwise tipping the guarder off that treats are imminent.

Exercise 3: This employs the identical format to Exercise 2 except now the guarder will have access to a previously guarded resource, such as a bone, toy, empty food dish or coveted sleeping location. Use the lowest value resource if there are clear gradations in the guarder's hierarchy.

As before, work or read, ignoring the dog for the first twenty minutes or so. It is very important that the treats be very valuable ones, high enough preferably to trump the resource. If the guarder does not engage the resource (i.e. ignores or walks away from it), don't worry. Do the exercise and remain alert as the resource may gain value when the other dog enters the room, especially if the other dog demonstrates any interest in it. To reduce the likelihood of this happening, place the resource away from the door.

For some guarders there are no low value resources – everything is guarded from the other dog. If the guarding has been mild, i.e. it takes a very close approach to elicit any threat, and the guarder has some protracted warnings in his or her "signature," go ahead with the exercise as described above. If the guarder is more explosive and there are no unguarded resources, use the largest possible room and station the guarder as far from the door as possible. Use a tether to ensure he doesn't migrate to another location that is more likely to spike proximity-induced guarding when the other dog is introduced to the room. Introduce the other dog on leash to maintain the distance. The resource should be within the guarder's radius, whether he engages it or not.

Repeat the exercise until you witness a clear CER to the entrance of the other dog. The guarder should be unreservedly more interested in the counter-stimulus, i.e. the bait he is going to receive, than the  resource. There should be some change denoting anticipation when the other dog enters, such as wagging, approaching the handler and sitting or orienting expectantly to where the food is expected to come from.

If you have been using tethering for the guarder and leash management for the other dog, once you have a clear CER, repeat another round of exercises without the tether, but retaining the leash on the other dog to prevent any proximity to the guarder and his prize. Guarding should not spike if you did the tethered version to the point of CER to the other dog's entrance. If it does, re-evaluate the previous exercise and/or make sure the guarder hasn't migrated too close to the door where the other dog is entering.

The next variation is a series of entrances that edge the other dog closer and closer to the guarder before the counter-stimulus party. It's wise to keep the other dog's interest in his treat to avoid him orienting to the guarder, as this can raise intensity too fast too soon for many guarders. When the guarder is relaxed and demonstrating an anticipatory CER to the other dog a couple of feet away, increase distance again but now cease wrangling the other dog and allow him or her to orient toward and look at the guarder. Proximity and orientation are variables that are independent often enough to warrant separating them in dog-dog hierarchies.

If eye contact proves volatile, it is worth the time and effort to work this variable intensively. Tether both dogs in a room at a sub-threshold distance for long intervals while you work. The guarder has a resource within radius. At occasional intervals, use your own body/voice or a lure to draw the eyes of the other dog to the guarder and his resource. Immediately open the bar for the guarder. If at any point the other dog looks away, close the bar. This can take a fair amount of repetition to isolate the other dog's gaze as the contingent stimulus for the treat bar, but is well worth the effort in dogs who find eye contact upsetting. Capitalize, when you can, on spontaneous gazes from non-guarder to guarder, as this removes your prompt as an earlier tip-off that the treat bar will soon open.

When the eye-contact obstacle is surmounted, allow the other dog to do room entrances off leash. The only exception here is if the other dog happens to be himself a guarder and one who furthermore threatens or attacks other dogs to get them off resources. If this is the case, work the original guarder with non-guarders off leash and work the pre-emptive striker separately before putting the two problem dogs together.

When the guarder has a good CER to the presence of the other dog off leash, even when the latter makes eye contact or orients toward the guarder, repeat exercises using the same level of resource but in different rooms in the house, from the point where the guarder is tethered and the other dog leashed. This usually goes quickly and smoothly.

Once there is relaxation and a CER to the other dog's off-leash presence in any room, recommence work with tether and leash using a higher value resource if one exists. I do not usually recommend going out of one's way to search for an extremely high value resource if this first round of exercises exhausts the main items the guarder's repertoire. Train for the items the dogs encounter in their day-to-day lives. An incredibly interesting and novel item is likely to spike guarding even in a nicely proofed dog, and often even in dogs that had no prior history of guarding. So, my standard recommendation is to manage for the rare, ultra-high value items. Simply give them to the dogs in separate rooms to avoid flare-ups. Thoroughly remove all trace of them before re-introducing the dogs.

Here is summary of the major hierarchy rungs:

1) Sitting dogs fed in sequence
2) Decrease distance if applicable
3) Room entrances without resources
4) Generalize to other rooms
5) Room entrances with unguarded resource present in guarder's radius (if everything guarded, must skip this)

6) Room entrances with guarded resource present, guarder tethered, other dog leashed
7) Guarder off tether, other dog leashed
8) Distance decreased, eye contact avoided
9) Distance increased, eye contact encouraged
10) Other dog off leash
11) Generalize other rooms from #5 on
12) Repeat hierarchy from #6 with higher value resources (if double resources both have completed hierarchies, combine them here starting from #6)
13) Cold trials – random, planned "management lapses" in day to day life
14) Maintenance – cold trials once per day (more often if guarding creeping back)

Operant Conditioning of Guarder

I think operant conditioning is a splendid alternative approach to resource guarding cases, largely because of the fluency most trainers already have with the nuances of this style of training. Well-executed operant techniques achieve a collateral CER, so the end result is similar to that achieved with D&C except that the guarder offers a response and feels happy and relaxed rather than just feeling happy and relaxed. When using operant conditioning on behaviors with strong emotional components, such as resource guarding, understanding of classical conditioning principles informs criteria decisions a great deal. As Bob Bailey notes, "Pavlov is on your shoulder" when you train, and nowhere more than when working on fear or aggression. A low rate of reinforcement will greatly reduce the collateral CER.

Dogs who are trained to sit, down, do tricks or other behaviors, develop CER's to salient aspects of the training stimulus package, e.g. the trainer, his or her hand reaches, bait pouch or other equipment used. This can be a "yippee" style CER if the training has been conducted with positive reinforcers or a fear CER ("oh-oh" with or without appeasement gestures) if the training involved aversives. In the case of resource guarding rehab, the presence of the other dog will be the contingent cue to do the behavior and be reinforced, so the CER will be very likely to become most strongly attached to the other dog. The net result is not only a behavior trained in that is mutually exclusive to guarding, but a warmer and fuzzier feeling about the other dog(s) around coveted resources.

To get started, you need a nicely polished behavior that is incompatible with guarding. Withdrawing is my favorite as it immediately self-negatively reinforces with distance from the other dog, allows the guarder to retain possession of the resource as well as collect the positive reinforcer you supply for compliance. The ideal indoors variation is to teach the guarder to exit the room, at first prompted by you and then cued by the entrance or proximity of the other dog.

For these exercises you need at least two rooms – the one the guarder is in and the one she will withdraw to. You also need good control of the stimulus dog to orchestrate entrances and to keep him from pursuing the guarder to the room she has withdrawn to. If there are not two rooms, work the rungs using "maximum distance" as the target rather than a room exit.

Exercise #1: Room Exit

First, practice cueing and then prompting the dog to go to the other room for food reinforcers. This is most efficiently accomplished as a targeting exercise, such as going to a specific spot like a dog bed in the other room from progressively further away, culminating in all the way from the next room. The food reinforcer can be at the target to begin and then supplied by the handler. Once the dog readily does this exercise, start practicing with the other (stimulus) dog's entrance as the initial cue. Remember there are no resources in the room yet. The sequence is now:

Stimulus dog enters ⟶ Guarder cued to exit ⟶
Guarder exits room ⟶ R+

It may be necessary to prompt a few times as the presence of the stimulus dog makes for a significantly different training picture. To engineer entrances by the stimulus dog, you may use an accomplice or else open and close the door, if the stimulus dog is obliging. The most important factor is that the stimulus dog not follow the guarder on her exit.

When the guarder readily exits on cue, and sometimes likely jumps the gun by exiting as soon as the stimulus dog appears, it's time to introduce the resource.

Exercise #2: Exit with Resource

The first way to practice this is without the stimulus dog present. Give the guarder a bone or toy that she has guarded in the past from the other dog. Shortly after she has engaged the object, cue the room exit as you did in Exercise 1. Three things could happen. The first is she does nothing. The second is she does the exit but leaves the resource behind and the third is she exits, bringing the resource with her. Our objective is the third one, the exit with the bone or toy. If you're lucky enough to get this right away, reinforce as usual and leave her with the resource in the target area. Practice several times to make sure the dog brings along the coveted object regularly.

If the dog does nothing, prompt by heading toward the door yourself, bending over and excitedly inviting her to do her targeting from the last exercise. If she is reluctant and dug in with the resource, I recommend practicing with a zero value object – basically a retrieve – before trying with a hot object again. If she does the room exit without the object, again, work it as a retrieve to the target room.

Once she is fluent at picking up her treasure and exiting to the target room with it, you can start practicing with the other dog present.

Exercise #3: Exit with Resource from Dog

You've practiced with the stimulus dog and with the resource separately. To combine them, set the guarder up as before with a previously guarded resource. Bring the stimulus dog into the room. If the stimulus dog has history of close approaches to the guarder in resource situations, leash him for these exercises until the guarder becomes fluent at her exit.

Once the stimulus dog is present and away from the door, cue and, if necessary, prompt the guarder to make her exit with the resource. If the stimulus dog is leashed, hook the leash onto something to prevent her meeting the guarder at the door or following her out. This exercise can take some wrangling so it can sometimes help to have another handler present. Practice several times in a row, re-orchestrating the original set-up each time. This artificiality will help get the behavior up and rolling in this much more difficult context. When it's slick, you can abandon this procedure and do only single cold trials. Don't quit rehearsing cold trials until the guarder exits readily on cue (i.e. without prompting).

Conditioning Dogs to Avoid Guarder

This is an easy, useful procedure and combines very nicely with either classical or operant conditioning of the guarder to afford a couple of lines of defense in a tense household.

It almost goes without saying that if you have to condition a dog to avoid a guarder, the reaction of the latter is obviously not a punishing event for the approaching dog. Luckily, straightforward operant conditioning comes to the rescue. The objective is to teach the approaching dog to withdraw and leave the guarder alone when he is eating, on a coveted sleeping location and/or has a bone or toy. If there are multiple scenarios, you may get generalized responding after working the first or you may have to work each in turn.

You can opt to teach the non-guarder to put distance between himself and the guarder on a cue from you or on a cue from the guarder. If the guarder does not offer a clear threat to use as a cue, such as growling or lip lifting, you are likely better off teaching him to withdraw on your cue.

As soon as the cue is given, be it from you ("leave her alone please") or the guarder, prompt the non-guarder to make tracks to a specified target, preferably in another room. Throw him a party with praise and treats and hang out with him there. It is much more difficult to get this behavior if you reward there but then yourself return to where the guarder was. When it is much stronger you can be less vigilant about your own positioning. For now, the spot away from the guarder is a destination for both of you to spend at least five minutes, even before the next rep.

It's also fine to practice cueing the non-guarder to this target at other times if you have opted to use a cue from you as the discriminative stimulus. As I mentioned, it's just usually not necessary. If there is more than one target area (i.e. the guarder sometimes occupies the usual target), practice both from likely locations. Once the behavior is strong in real contexts, I'd advise reserving reinforcing it except at these times. The narrowed stimulus control has a better chance of leading to more automatic exits. Let me explain.

If you diligently practice this exercise, you will usually find the non-guarder withdrawing from the guarder prior to the cue, which is fine. He learns that in the context of the guarder with a resource, the cue usually comes and anticipates it. In this case, the anticipation is equally reinforceable as it really pre-empts confrontation between the two dogs.

For this procedure, it is usually possible to work straight away in vivo, i.e. in actual guarding situations. Depending on the explosiveness and thresholds of the guarder, it may be necessary to have worked her first. In cases where management, i.e. avoidance of dramatic threat displays, can be achieved while the non-guarder is trained, the order does not matter. I also know of cases where only the non-guarder was worked and this produced a satisfactory result for the client.

Sibling Rivalry

I am using the term sibling rivalry to refer to aggression occurring between dogs in the same household, whether or not they are related and whether or not it is necessarily "rivalry." The decision to intervene, as with resource guarding, is usually based on fight severity, i.e. ABI, and frequency. Occasional disagreements between dogs in the same household are inevitable.

Most cases can be resolved by using the techniques already described. There is very commonly a combination of resource competition – the owner, coveted spots along and/or bones and toys – and proximity sensitivity. It could be that the proximity sensitivity, when it exists is acquired through repeated bouts of resource guarding, rather than being secondary to impoverished early socialization. The tip-off is a gradual onset in dogs who formerly got along well. Getting along well means affiliativeness – greeting each other after separations – as well as some play.

Proximity sensitivity can also be secondary to discomfort around dogs. Such a dog living with another dog may habituate to that dog's presence yet not tolerate his or her close contact or play solicitation. And, finally, socialized dogs without strong resource issues also frequently have demonstrable preferences among their dog associates. It is not surprising that not all dogs that live together necessarily like each other.

Squabbling between dogs within the same household is most commonly interpreted by owners as the result of jostling for dominance. Solutions stemming from this interpretation will involve measures such as "supporting the hierarchy" by doling out important resources to the presumed higher-ranking animal. From a conditioning perspective, this could be inefficient, as often the presumed dominant animal is the one behaving more aggressively and therefore in greater need of learning that attention, cookies and bones to the other dog *predict* attention, cookies and bones for him or herself.

Predation and Predatory Drift

Predation is food acquisition rather than agonistic or defensive behavior, however the results – distressed owners and dogs and, in particular here, serious injuries – warrant careful attention. There are some key divisions to do with the targets, presence or not of any social behavior and whether the dog has killed or severely injured other dogs (is a "finisher").

Dogs sometimes display frank predatory behavior toward other dogs the same way they might toward squirrels, cats and other critters. Such dogs may direct regular social behavior toward dogs on other occasions or confine their predation to small dogs, or running dogs only. Each dog will have a profile, broad or narrow, of the targeted dogs.

I am going to defer discussion of severe cases where there is no social behavior whatsoever to the next section, on compulsive fighting, as the management and interventions (and, speculatively, the etiology) are the same.

Dogs that have a narrow target range – small dogs, especially when running or scurrying (retired racer syndrome) – are best managed, whether or not they are known finishers. The risk of injury is too high, the behavior harder than most to modify and the management usually easy to implement. There is also some risk of predatory drift (see below), even in the case of habitual non-finishers.

An equally serious but less well-known phenomenon is that of predatory drift, which is the kicking in of predatory reflexes in an interaction that begins as a social interaction. As opposed to regular predation, which happens predictably when a dog with an identified predatory predisposition is exposed to one of his targets, predatory drift can occur among non-identified dogs who had never been predatory before and may never be again after. It kicks in because of specific contextual triggers. The riskiest contexts are:

❑ Play or a squabble between two dogs that are extremely different in size – the smaller dog panics, yelps and/or struggles. The simulation of a prey item is so close that the roles in the interaction drift from a social scuffle to predator-prey. The greater the size disparity, the greater the risk, for a couple of reasons. Firstly, the likelihood of the smaller dog getting inadvertently stepped on or otherwise

105

ouched, even in a normal play session with a reasonably gentle dog, is greater if the dog in question is really tiny. Secondly, I would speculate that the tinier the dog, the better the simulation of a prey item to the bigger dog. And, thirdly, the ease with which the larger dog can grab and shake the smaller one goes up as size difference increases. Grab and shake is often present in predatory drift incidents. Most of us have seen dogs grab and shake toys. Even if non-lethal pressure is exerted, a grab and shake inflicted on a small dog can break its neck.

❑ Two or more dogs engaging in intense play, chase or a scuffle with a dog that begins to panic, yelp and/or struggle. Dogs have also been known to attack injured dogs and this effect is also facilitated by the attacking unit being two or more dogs as opposed to one.

Because predatory drift can occur in dogs without any particular history, all owners and practitioners should exercise some diligence in the two contexts above – large to small interactions and "double team" (two+ Vs. one). While it is quite true that many such interactions are completely benign, predatory drift is common enough that most dog people have either witnessed it or know someone who has. The risks multiply if both factors are present. Another obvious factor that increases risk is the involvement of a known predatory dog in the mix, especially a finisher.

Compulsive Fighting

When there is a complete absence of any normal social behavior and severe, unstoppable fighting when access is provided to any dog, I'm calling it compulsive fighting. It is most commonly seen in game-bred pitbulls and other fighting breeds. Many game-bred dogs are not compulsive fighters and demonstrate social behavior such as investigation and play. The propensity to fight is usually elevated by social maturity and the fighting style, once the dog is engaged, is extremely characteristic. Rather than expending significant energy in the rituals of noise and flashing teeth or inflicting single bite releases, game-bred dogs have a more predatory fighting style (i.e. grab and shakes and deep, hard bites), very much like a terrier with game.

Rehab of such dogs is not generally attempted, though some pit rescuers have successfully integrated game dogs into multi-dog households. All stress that the dogs should be supervised at all times when together and to expect ready fighting. Kim Moeller of The San Francisco SPCA's Behavior and Training Department worked a game dog over a six month period and got not only cessation of attacking but essentially normal social behavior, including investigation and play. The dog was adopted out carefully and, as of this writing (two years post adoption), is maintaining its gains.

The technique used centered around mechanically preventing fighting by use of muzzles, Gentle Leader headcollars, lines and leashes and using the time bought to establish a CER, first to familiar, passive dogs and later to novel and more outgoing, active dogs. Warm-up also turned out to be a useful variable in this case.

Prevention of Dog-Dog Aggression

There are a number of measures that owners, dog professionals and public officials could take to reduce the incidence of intra-specific aggression in dogs.

For Owners

- ❑ Nursery Puppy Classes
- ❑ Regular Puppy Classes
- ❑ Regular Play Sessions
- ❑ Early Intervention if Problems Arise

If you have a puppy, one of the best favors you can do him is to take him to a puppy class. Such a class should include carefully supervised and orchestrated off-leash play sessions. All the puppies in the class should be vaccinated and should be puppies rather than juvenile or older dogs (i.e. no adult canine teeth should have yet erupted). All training techniques should employ strictly the starting and stopping of praise, food, play and toys; there should be no use of aversives such as collar corrections, shaking, striking, spraying with water or startle.

The age group that are considered prime fodder for puppy classes are the 12 – 18 week olds. There is some building consensus among dog trainers, especially those that treat adult behavior problems, that earlier attendance at classes may be much more beneficial, i.e. among the 7 to 11 week olds. The immunization status of puppies in that age group is poor, as passive immunity from maternal antibodies is on the wane and active immunity from vaccines not yet achieved. So, the standard recommendation has been to sequester puppies from other dogs until they have had at least a couple of boosters. This means puppies under 11 or 12 weeks, and often even older, can't attend class.

When the risk from relinquishment or euthanasia due to behavior problems is considered, the case for re-visiting the prohibition from classes is reasonable. The soundest objective is a prudent balance between disease risk and missed opportunity to socialize and train the puppy as well as educate the owner early in the game afforded by class attendance. Factors to consider in an individual case include prevalence of the most easily transmitted diseases, such as parvovirus, in the local population, the breed of dog (both from disease susceptibility and fear/aggression susceptibility standpoints), screening of class participants and class premises hygiene and disinfection. Fully informed owner consent to either take or forego early training and socialization and its attendant disease risk will eventually become the norm.

After a puppy becomes a juvenile and then a sexually mature adult, most dog behavior experts agree that there is still some social development. It is also probable that social skills – ease with which the dog delivers and reads the subtler body language during interactions with other dogs – remain most fluent when rehearsed. For this reason, socialization opportunities for adult dogs should be sought on a regular basis. For some, trips to dog parks or day care are part of the fabric of their day-to-day lives. For others, however, there may be suburban solitude or a more static dog network that keeps certain relationships and "play ruts" well greased but few or no meet and greets with novel dogs.

If you are a dog owner and your dog fights, bullies, is difficult to manage on leash or seems uncomfortable around other dogs, get yourself into the hands of a competent professional. The more time that goes by without intervention, the more worn down you are, the worse your dog's PR problems are, the more entrenched the problem may be, and the greater the chance of some fluke or mishap that dictates placement or euthanasia. The same goes for problems in multi-dog households. Even if you have some training or behavior experience, it may be worth it to get an objective set of eyes on your situation.

For Dog Professionals

- ❑ Pre-Puppy Screening and Education
- ❑ Breeder Intervention
- ❑ Wider Availability and Better Marketing of Puppy Kindergarten Classes
- ❑ Partnering with Veterinarians to Achieve Widely Available and Hygienic Nursery Classes
- ❑ Public Education on Non-Aversive Training
- ❑ Meet & Greets as Part of Class Curricula

Given the bogglingly wide range of interest in preparedness training for life events such as getting married or having a child, efforts at getting pre-puppy education to catch on will likely impact the high end of the dog-acquiring continuum. Nevertheless, it's an outstanding idea, as once a puppy actually materializes, most owners lose considerable available executive function to the twin sinks of oxytocin poisoning ("she's so CUUUUTE!!!!") and the entropy secondary to urine, feces, puppy biting et al.

Pre-puppy planning encompasses house preparation, gear purchasing, some thought about routine and rules that will be in place from the get-go and, in some programs, rehearsal of the mechanics of basic training techniques on older, quieter dogs. It can also function as breed or type counseling, i.e. what breed or type of dog is the best match for a given person or family, and go so far as to explore whether the party should be considering a dog at all.

Pre-puppy screening for dog-dog is partly a socialization assault planning session and partly an odds-playing game where, depending on the stated priority level of good dog relations (e.g. they already have a dog, they love going to dog parks, intend to put the dog in day-care etc.), the counselor will steer the client toward or away from breeds, lines or, possibly, individuals.

Breeder intervention after the decision has been reached about which specimens' DNA to combine is most critical in the case of a singleton puppy or a puppy without playmates due to quarantine or other circumstances. Animal shelters frequently find themselves in the position of housing litters, partial litters and singleton puppies between 3 and 8 weeks of age, so vital for normal social development. Hand-reared puppies might logically be at higher risk for serious dog-dog problems in later life, and it is unknown whether any such effect would be mitigated by puppy class play sessions, of either the kindergarten (12-18) or nursery (7-11) variety. In the absence of research to answer these questions, the most prudent course of action for a breeder or shelter— is to develop a network of other puppy sources for those times when a singleton is in their care. Playmates should be as close in age as possible and co-housing is the ideal so that interactions can run the gamut from sleeping, eating and hanging out together rather than simply getting together for play time.

Puppy classes have become enormously popular, a most gratifying trend. There are still corners where they are not available, or where old-style jerk & praise style obedience classes are marketed as puppy classes. And, although no one knows the exact percentage of puppy owners who attend class, it's far from a majority. Better marketing is needed for puppy classes to be seen as a universal necessity in a sensible society.

CONDOMS	SEATBELTS	BICYCLE HELMETS	PUPPY CLASS

Owners also benefit enormously from being prepared ahead of time for such phenomena as possible targeting of adolescent or "bulls-eye" dogs, diminished playfulness, increased selectiveness and lower tolerance for rudeness in other dogs as their seemingly unflappable puppies mature.

If nursery puppy classes are to become widespread, I think veterinarians will need to be involved, at the very least to bless the concept and at most, to partner with trainers to get puppies in. Veterinarians are in a unique position in a community to monitor where puppies who turn up sick have been – and therefore be able to steer owners away from establishments that are not screening or cleaning adequately.

Amazingly, in 2004, there is still discussion in some professional circles about the advisability of hurting dogs to train them. It's not remarkable then that the public is lagging even further behind. The likelihood is that eventually the deliberate infliction of pain, startle or discomfort to motivate dogs will be illegal; however, in the interim mass public education would remove significant pressure from trainers who must waste energy daily trying to convince owners, one by one, to try gentler tools and methods. There are occasional PSA's on TV about spaying and neutering, so perhaps sound bites about aversives-free training and behavior modification may one day appear. While arguments can be made regarding the efficacy of aversives for motivating obedience type behaviors and building fear and avoidance, it is much more difficult to argue their usefulness when the objective is to change an existing negative emotional response. If dogs feel threatened, uncomfortable, defensive or afraid, the side effects of pain or startle are exacerbating.

If you do regular leash walks with your dog, you have probably noticed how few dog owners are able to handle an on-leash dog-dog meeting. They avoid meeting dogs altogether by crossing the street or otherwise giving a wide berth and, when meetings are allowed, there is a great deal of mechanical control, most notably a shortened and/or tightened leash. It's not surprising, however, as they aren't born knowing how to do this. Many owners do take training classes and these would be a great place to teach and rehearse the basic maneuvers for dog encounters: checking in with other owner, approaching with loose leash, monitoring body language for flags, facilitating mutual (circle) investigations, breaking off cheerily, emergency escapes if things turn awry, and being vigilant on the inside while broadcasting a jolly demeanor.

For Public Officials

- ❑ Accountability for Dog Breeders
- ❑ Resources for Anti-Dogfighting Enforcement
- ❑ Dog Parks
- ❑ Backyard Dog Initiatives

The issue of accountability for dog breeders is one that is germane to all aggression, not just dog-dog. Consider the following. Although it is against the law to build a bomb in my basement, regardless of who may then buy it or transport it somewhere to go off, it is perfectly legal to deliberately combine dog genes to achieve the highest possible aggressiveness, advertise it as an aggressive dog, and then sell it to someone who could then be held liable should the dog ever bite someone, while there are no legal ramifications for me, the breeder. The law deduces motive all the time in criminal matters on the basis of preponderance (or other standards) of evidence. In those cases where it can be ascertained that an individual deliberately bred an aggressive dog, why are they not held accountable when the dog offends?

Part of the reason lies in the Standard Social Science Model (SSSM) of behavior that has guided human sociology and psychology for several decades. For well-meaning political reasons, the contribution of genetics to behavior has been too hot a potato, and so the model of an absolute or nearly absolute tabula rasa has become official doctrine. SSSM ideas have influenced public policy toward dogs as well – it's not the dog's "fault," it's how he was raised/trained/not trained/abused/neglected that is to blame, i.e. the owner's fault. Aside from the unsupportable stance that genes do not influence behavior, it's not the dog's "fault" either that he has been bred for characteristics that make it more likely he will harm someone at some point.

An obvious example is pitbulls. Decades of breeding for intense, efficient and persevering aggression toward other dogs has resulted in a dog that is, unastonishingly, often extremely aggressive to other dogs. Similarly, decades of breeding for "aloofness," "wariness of strangers," "one-man" or "one-family" dogs has resulted in, equally obviously, breeds that are harder to socialize – they're fine with familiar people but much less comfortable around novel social stimuli. Breeders then expect owners to compensate with extensive socialization, rather than contributing another line of defense by selectively breeding for sociability. If we really want fewer dog bites, redundancy is a good place to start. Genes *and* rearing.

114

Dogfighting is rampant in urban centers and animal control and welfare officials can only crack down on this scourge as their resources permit. Funds to support enforcement of existing laws and lobby for stiffer penalties and greater powers for animal welfare officers are chronically short. There is also the deeper question of what causes disenfranchised people – most commonly young men – to get a rush out of watching dogs fight flat out. Aside from the grim lives and deaths of the dogs that are exploited in pit fights, non-fighting stock and many of their puppies end up in the hands of backyard breeders and ultimately, pouring into animal shelters and rescue organizations.

There is a wide variety of availability of dog parks in the US and Canada, with some municipalities having them without issue, and some having them, nearly having them or not having them but with some heated discord between owners and non-owners. There is no question that they represent a net benefit for most young dogs as far as exercise opportunity and mental stimulation. Dogs have complex social lives and brains that evolved to handle this. Navigating a dog social scene is an enrichment activity that is hard to match. Given the epidemic of behavior problems that benefit from increased exercise and stimulation, dog parks are a wonderful thing. From a dog-dog perspective, off-leash interaction with a wide variety of dogs is the best track to maximize a dog's social skills. The only caveats to dog park use are:

1. Monitoring for bullying and play skill deficits and

2. Human courtesy and respect

Left untreated, bullying and play skill deficits are often progressive at dog parks. Such dogs can be quite psychologically damaging to certain other dogs and, depending on ABI and degree of roughness, physically damaging. They are also PR nightmares for dogs in general.

In the case of normal range interactions, posturing and squabbling, a different phenomenon, that of *human* bullying, is often in evidence. What this usually looks like is someone expressing discomfort or alarm at witnessing some dog interaction and then being steamrolled by nearby quasi dog experts who scornfully inform them that this is natural and normal. While it may (or may not) be, the lack of basic respect or kindness is something that has never failed to dismay me whenever I have witnessed it.

Finally, it is difficult to imagine a sadder life than that of backyard dogs. Their plight is the result of some combination of entrenched thinking that somehow that's where dogs of a certain size belong and/or are happier and the vicious cycle of the dog never learning house manners and so behaving badly if ever allowed in and so being further relegated to what is basically the existence of livestock. The latter effect is compounded by the social deprivation, which produces hyper-motivation and extremely over the top behavior whenever the dog does get visited, convincing the owner that the dog would be a disaster in the house.

Among some backyard dogs, the epidemic of fence fighting is exacerbated by a virtual complete absence of walks. The yard functions conveniently as exercise, fresh air and bathroom, ostensibly removing the inconvenience of having to give the dog any minor change in scenery. I hope in my lifetime to see a shift in the popularity of backyard dogs.